The Fiery Canon

I dedicate this book to Hilary with love and gratitude.

Front cover image – Peter Capron, 2012

The Fiery Canon

The Ramblings of a Rustic Rector

David Capron

First published by
History Into Print, 56 Alcester Road,
Studley, Warwickshire B80 7LG in 2012
www.history-into-print.com

Reprinted October 2012
Reprinted August 2016

ISBN: 978-1-85858-341-9

A Cataloguing in Publication Record
for this title is available from the British Library.

Typeset in Baskerville
Printed in Great Britain by
4edge Ltd.

CONTENTS

ACKNOWLEDGEMENTS: PAST AND PRESENT

Blessed John Henry Cardinal Newman. The Spirit of Vatican 2. Reverend Canon Raymond Hammer: Theologian who encouraged me to raise my academic game. Bishop John Daly, formerly Bishop of Gambia, Gold Coast and Korea who instilled a missionary zeal! Liz Ford, P.A. to the Diocesan Secretary who just said that I ought to record my stories. Cath Tomlinson, Deacon of Alcester Baptist Church for encouragement in all matters relating to IT. Reverend Richard Dobell, my dear friend and colleague, so tragically taken from all of us. All the Churchwardens who I have served with over the years and especially in respect of these last seven years, the wisdom imparted to me by both Marion Deeks and Chris Wright. For the first time ever, my wardens have been younger than me! It is clearly time for me to retire.

The cover design is a representation of the banners carried by the Pilgrimage of Grace in 1536, following the preaching of a sermon in Louth, County of Lincoln. This was a mass protest against the suppression of the monasteries by Henry VIII. It was not so much a complaint against the King, but a desire to restore the pastoral ministry of the church, upon which so many people of very limited means, so much depended. It was brutally put down by a mixture of terror, deceit and violence. The banner displays the five wounds of Christ, which today represent the five marks of mission, namely:

1. To proclaim the Good News of the Kingdom.
2. To teach, baptise and nurture new believers.
3. To respond to human need by loving service.
4. To seek to transform unjust structures of Society.
5. To strive to safeguard the integrity of creation and sustain and renew the life of the earth.

FOREWORD BY THE RIGHT REVEREND DOCTOR CHRISTOPHER COCKSWORTH, BISHOP OF COVENTRY

David Capron has had a long association with Bishops of Coventry. Ordained by the illustrious Cuthbert Bardsley, David has served under five Coventry bishops in total, with me as the latest. So it is a great privilege to be asked to write a foreword to the account of a life, so much of it spent in the Diocese of Coventry as a schoolboy, then, between leaving school at Rugby and training for ordained ministry, bank clerk, insurance salesman and refuse collector; then, for very many years, deacon and priest, in a number of parishes. Indeed, apart from his training at Salisbury and Wells Theological College, and a notable period as vicar of Newton Aycliffe in the Diocese of Durham, David has spent his adult life in the Diocese. As you can imagine, Father Capron has become quite an institution in this bit of the country!

The life of a Church of England vicar – or rector (it amounts to pretty much the same thing) - remains a source of fascination to the British public. The success of the recent BBC serial 'Rev' is clear testimony both to the curiosity that people have about this enigmatic role in community life, and the affection that parish clergy retain in the hearts of so many, despite their, at best, tangential contact with the Church. Maybe one of the reasons for this is that capable priests like David Capron create lots of those tangential points of encounter with the Church and its clergy. I do not just mean 'the hatching, matching and dispatching' that David recounts, often hilariously, but also those manifold ways of getting under the skin of local communities through their clubs, societies, leisure pursuits and the like.

David has excelled in this sort of community involvement. He has turned his love of sport, the fire services and good ale to great effect. If there was not a rugby club to join, he founded one. If there was not a scout group to support, he began one. The Fire Service has always been in his bones through his father's distinguished career and David found ways to serve in his own impressive way as a longstanding chaplain. Ale, with its accompanying sociality and conviviality, has figured prominently in David's ministry, no doubt breaking down many (almost entirely, in my experience, false) stereotypes of party-pooper clergy.

Through this sort of embeddedness in community life, David – like other clergy at their best – has helped towns and villages to regard themselves highly. His love of the place and people he has served has shown that *that* community counts and is worth nurturing. The remarkable festivities in Alcester on St Nicholas Day (the patron saint of its parish church) are an example of the sort of celebration of local life that the Church can inspire when well led. Equally, the practical care and priestly pastoring that David was able to give to the Warwickshire Fire Service as it suffered surely one of the most harrowing times of its history, only happened because he had built up banks of trust through his long years of presence in quieter times.

Behind David's energetic ministry there have been two sustaining forces. One is Hilary, who has supported David with grace and wisdom for much of his ministry and built with him a fine family. As you will see, David has dedicated this book to her 'with love and gratitude'. That says it all. The other is David's disciplined devotional life: commitment to the Daily Office, love of the Eucharist, celebration of Saints' Days. These ancient patterns of the spiritual life have enabled David to stay close to his Lord and ready to serve him wherever he was called. 'I would not have wanted to be anything other than a priest', says David to his readers at the end of his life-story. *David*, on behalf of us all and especially, if I may, of the bishops with whom you have ministered, we are glad and grateful that you heard God's call and that you have ministered God's grace so faithfully. Your stipendiary ministry may be drawing to a close but you will remain a priest called to bring God's blessing to the world, so I end my foreword with the same words Cuthbert spoke to you at your ordination, 'May God accomplish his work that he hath begun in you, through Jesus Christ our Lord'. *Amen!*

+ *Christopher Coventry*

INTRODUCTION

I am not really sure why I actually decided that I wanted to write a book. The kernel of an idea came to me some years ago when I discovered that I had a famous poet as an ancestor. But lack of literary inspiration changed my thinking to the idea of gathering up some of his poems and then republishing them; in other words a little bit of cheating! I never really got down to it and other than a visit to Bideford Library, where a large portrait of Edward Capern is displayed, nothing happened until I discovered that a very distant relation had beaten me to it with her own publication.

Then there was the move to Alcester with its Barchester connotations and the feeling that the least likely thing to happen would in fact be the most likely! Such a scenario deserves a book, albeit from a Rector who had struggled with academia at all levels. The temptation has proved irresistible and with retirement beckoning at the end of 2012, it was a question of now or never. What has amazed me is that I have done it, and also without too much aggro from within me. I started off with voice recognition software, but I got myself into such a mess both with that mode of writing and also with the computer filing system, that I took advice and decided to do it the hard way. There are so many other stories that I could tell but I think you will have to ask me for aural texts as I doubt very much that there will be the demand for a sequel. In any case what would I call it?

So, I am just going to allow myself the space for a brief reflection before signing off.

I look back on over 36 years in Holy Orders. I was ordained according to the rites of the Book of Common Prayer and I am glad of that. Not for me some wishy washy concoctions, with the good old BCP you knew where you stood! I cannot see me doing anything differently and I have been decidedly fortunate throughout my ministry, especially with my wife Hilary, sons Mark, Peter and Stephen, daughter-in-law, Helen and grandsons, Joel and Nathan. God always knew where he wanted me and my trip to the Kingdom of Northumbria is very much a case in point. What will I do with myself in retirement? I hope to see a lot more of Shottery

RFC, to travel by train whenever I can, to spend some time bird watching and to do a lot of walking. I shall also need to find a spiritual home, which might be a little difficult for me with my churchmanship background.

I have rambled enough and so will finish off with two quotations:

"Great things are not done by those who sit down and count the cost of every thought and action." Spoken by Sir Daniel Gooch as a tribute to Isambard Kingdom Brunel.

"Persons influence us, Voices melt us, Looks subdue us, Deeds inflame us." Good old Newman in his Grammar of Ascent.

These two quotations continue to live with me and inspire me. I hope they will do the same for you.

Per Crucem

Feast of the Ascension 2012

Chapter 1

EARLY BEGINNINGS

The Capron family are of Huguenot extraction and came to Tiverton in the 1800s, if not earlier. A cursory glance at the Parish records shows that the spelling tended to vary dependent on the hearing of the verger/sexton! Capern (The birdseed makers), Caporn, Capon were spread liberally across the register and yet it was clear to me that they were all from the same family. The family were weavers, in fact the family name comes from the word – Cape. It did not take too long for the family to set up shop as perfumers in Tiverton and then there is record of movement to Barnstaple where a certain Edward Capern, who was the local postman, achieved national importance as a poet of distinction whose verses evoked happy memories of country lanes and country pursuits. He also wrote poetry which soldiers found to be especially patriotic and many a fallen warrior was found to have a copy of Capern's poems on his body after the battle. Edward Capern moved in very high poetic circles and was warmly compared with Robbie Burns; he kept in close contact with other well known poets and when he died, he was granted the honour of a state funeral, which presumably means that the Government of the day, paid for all expenses. He was buried in the churchyard at Heaton Punchardon and his postman's bell is set into the tombstone.

I have not yet established how the Caprons arrived in Minehead, but they certainly came from Tiverton and set up business as engineers, specialising in sanitary and water supply matters. Needless to say it did not take long for the family to take more than a passing interest in the extinguishment of fires! Four generations served the Minehead Fire Brigade with my father ending up as Chief Fire Officer of Warwickshire. The story goes that on one particular Sunday, Divine service was in progress at St. Michaels Church on the hill, when fire broke out at the local bakery. The shout went up, "Call the fire brigade" and then there was a wait until the sound of hooves was heard and the local lads arrived to expeditiously put out the blaze, to the evident satisfaction of the West Somerset Free Press which praised the work of John Capron and his merry men. On another famous occasion, there was a turn out to which both Minehead and Williton brigades were summoned; needless to say, Minehead got there first, basically because they had a fully mechanised appliance, whereas poor old Williton had to get the horses out of the stable.

It did not take long for the business to set up a garage and was the first to sell petrol in that part of the West Country. The family also got into selling bicycles and it is fascinating to look at the beautifully inscribed ledgers which show the daily routine of the business. My father told the story that while on leave he manned the pumps and served a very important personage: i.e. the Archbishop of Canterbury, Geoffrey Fisher. My father, who remained a devout Roman Catholic to the day that he died, was more than happy with a ten shilling tip! That was serious money in those days, especially down in the depths of West Somerset.

Dad started his fire brigade career as a call boy. When the phone rang, my grandfather would kick him out of bed and dad would cycle round Minehead, turning out the retained crew before going back to get hold of his father, who was the Chief. It was about this time that my mother moved to Minehead from South Wales.

The Cooper family were big supporters of the Co-op movement and needless to say, they were convinced socialists. My maternal grandfather used to be manager of the store in Resolven, which is in the Neath valley, but the family lived in Glyn-neath which is just up the valley. I can remember going to visit some distant relatives near Swansea and calling on the old neighbour. I was highly delighted because he had been a top rugby union player called Glyn Prosser who had played for Neath and Wales. He was a mighty man with massive hands who had worked in the pits, but was remembered nationally for being part of the great Welsh team which included Wilf Wooler and defeated the All Blacks.

My mother was one of six children, four girls and two boys; unfortunately both brothers died before the war and correct mourning was observed. My mother was the eldest and therefore the first to go out with boys. When my father took her out for the first time, Dad, in a somewhat unusually undiplomatic style, decided to list his pet hates. First, it was the Welsh and secondly it was the Co-op movement. When Dad brought my mother back to her house, she stood firmly erect and informed my father that she was Welsh, and proud of it, also Daddy was manager of the Co-op and not a red under the bed. I was never sure how I ever got into this world!

My parents married in 1941 and I came along in 1945. I can always say that I was conceived in war (Selworthy, I am told), and born in peace. Unfortunately my baptism was far from peaceful and took place in the local R.C. church. My mother was not allowed to hold me and she subsequently stormed out, only to be brought back by one of my two sets of Godparents. I only found out some years later that I had two sets; one to keep the church happy and another set to satisfy my parents and especially my mother. The problem was that my paternal grandmother was a strong Roman Catholic who toed the party line. She was a convert from congregationalism and therefore totally unyielding. My father was much more laid back in these matters, but there were ramifications when I was about to be ordained all those years later when I needed documentary proof of my baptism.

We stayed in Minehead until 1948 when the National Fire Service was being disbanded. I don't really remember those early years, but I was told plenty of stories. Especially during one of the first Remembrance Day parades. Naturally the armed forces took pride of place, but the Fire Brigade had reckoned that they would come next as the fourth arm. Unfortunately that was not to be and the Firemen were told that they could parade as long as they went to the back (memories of Dad's Army)! My grandfather was having none of it and quite bluntly said that "he was not marching behind the bloody Brownies" and promptly marched the firemen off and back to the station. I am told that this tradition ran in the family and when my father was Chief of Warwickshire he took exactly the same line. Little did he know that his future daughter-in-law would become a Divisional Commissioner for the Guide Movement. I don't really remember my grandfather, other than him driving me around in his little car with me standing on the passenger seat; he chose to brake very suddenly and I disappeared from sight. I suppose he hoped that I would follow in the Capron tradition of engineering and car repairs so he gave me a Meccano set for my sixth birthday, not knowing that I would go into the church, an institution which he held to be suspect!

So, my memories of Minehead are based on the experience of holidays and occasional visits. The drama of Exmoor, the delight of Minehead

Harbour, the fun of the West Somerset Railway and above all, the challenging, brooding and majestic power of Dunkery Beacon. I belong to the Exmoor Society and to the W.S.R. as well as somewhat more speculatively, to the Lynton and Barnstaple Railway. Whenever I return, we usually stay at the Northfield Hotel on the North Hill or the Luttrell Arms in Dunster and that gives us the opportunity to go out walking. The North Hill has its particular attractions, especially when you get over to Selworthy Beacon with the dramatic view of Porlock Bay. However, my favourite walk is to start at Horner water and walk up the valley before climbing up towards Stoke Pero and then approaching Dunkery from the west. There is then the chance to soak up the view and, weather permitting, to look over the Bristol Channel towards Wales. The return to Horner water involves passing by Webbers Post where you can look back up to Dunkery and admire it in all its many moods.

So we moved to Woodstock in Oxfordshire where dad was appointed Deputy and I went to the local village school. The school was next door to the railway station which served a branch line to Kidlington. It was the old fashioned push and pull with the added attraction that on Saturdays there was a through train to Oxford. Unfortunately the line was closed on March 1st 1952 and they placed detonators on the line for the last train, I remember it so well. I also remember the weekly collection by the Lavender Cart (emptying out the privies) and Remembrance Sunday when the Home Guard always paraded and their commanding officer looked distinctly like Captain Mainwaring!

I loved my time in Woodstock, we lived opposite the Parish Church in a building which is now the County Museum. We also had a good view of the Bear Hotel which frequently saw important guests, so we tended to hang around outside in the hope of seeing someone famous. Blenheim Park was next door and the grounds were my play area. At that time television was making a comeback after the war and I remember walking down the Oxford Road with my mother who wanted to buy some honey from one of the big houses there. There was a television which was switched on and I was invited to sit down and watch it. It did not take too long to persuade my father and we had one installed just in time for the Coronation. All sorts of friends turned up and there was quite a party which spilled out to join with all sorts of other parties. There were sports events and the usual traditional fair. But the day of the Coronation brought atrocious weather and buckets of rain. I can still clearly see Queen Salote of Tonga in her open carriage and positively refusing to be covered up. The crowds loved her.

My father entered into the spirit of local life and he played cricket in the summer, while my mother inhabited the tennis club. They both went to whist drives and Dad was out at nights quite a bit, visiting retained stations and giving talks to W.I. Clubs and Village Hall Committees. There was great excitement on one occasion when it was decided to film part of the "Titfield Thunderbolt" in Woodstock. It was all outside our house and I had a first rate view of a "train" coming up Park Street.

There was also great family anticipation, because Dad had been threatening to score his first half century for Blenheim Park Cricket Club. Being the wicketkeeper, he didn't always get a chance, but I was up there when he pulled it off and I still have the bat to this day. Cricket was played on the lawns in front of the Palace, there were no changing facilities, so you changed in the box hedge; eventually they got permission from His Grace to put up a tent, on the understanding that it was taken down after each match. There were also fire service games as well, and in the summer it never rained and the holidays seemed to last for an eternity. Oh happy days. Would it ever end? 1957 saw me leave the village school and go to the big School at Chipping Norton and suddenly the world was very much bigger.

Chapter 2

SECONDARY SCHOOL

Chipping Norton was literally a breath of fresh air; very fresh air in fact because this old Cotswold Mill town was at least 700 feet up and there was quite a long bus journey in the morning to get there. Cross country runs were littered by springs of water which popped up everywhere and snow blizzards were commonplace. On one occasion it took more than four hours to get home as the wind had created havoc with countless snow drifts and to make matters worse, it was the old fashioned type of bus with no doors to protect passengers from the bitter cold. I remember that we struggled to a transport cafe nearby after we had become stuck and warmed ourselves up with hot tea. Fortunately my parents got through from Woodstock, by which time traffic was beginning to move again and I had a ride home in a warm car.

What I didn't realise when I was at Chipping Norton was that despite having taken and passed the 11+ exam, the School had become a comprehensive, not that I minded. There was a rough and ready attempt to join up with the secondary modern school down the road. We joined up for games, the boys joined up for woodwork and the girls joined up for domestic science. My headmaster in my first term was the fearsome Paddy Martin who we used to see swinging his stick as he walked back to the Head's house for lunch. We all reckoned that he was practising the use of the cane! But interestingly, I met up with Paddy some years later when he was appointed Headmaster of Warwick School. By then he had become a licensed reader and he invited me to preach for him in Chapel. It was good to see him again, but he still had that formidable air about him. But my morning trips by bus were soon to end, because Dad landed the post of Assistant Chief Fire Officer of Warwickshire and so we moved to Rugby, which I thought was in the far and distant lands of the north. It wasn't long before people were moving to Rugby and commuting by train to London.

Education needed to be sorted out so I was enrolled at Lawrence Sheriff Grammar School which was known as the Lower School to Rugby School down the road. The Chairman of the Governors was the Headmaster of Rugby School and the Headmaster of the Grammar School was usually a senior teacher from the Upper School. Needless to say there was an inverted snobbery about these things and most parents were delighted to send their sons to the "Lower School"! The school was voluntary aided because it took some of the investment income upon which Rugby School depended. Lawrence Sheriff had been a master grocer in London and his bequest included the land in Holborn on which the HQ of the Prudential Assurance Company is to be found. Quite a tidy sum. But leaving that aside, although it was only for one year, I did enjoy myself there. Somehow or other I won an organ scholarship which produced weekly lessons free of charge. However I did have to struggle a bit in one department and that was Latin, because Chipping Norton did not teach Latin in the first year, but Lawrence Sheriff did. This was where there was a fundamental change brewing for me. I needed to learn a whole year of Latin in half a term, which actually happened. Having got back on the level, the tutor offered to take me on for the Common Entrance Exam for Rugby. My parents were delighted at the prospect especially as the tutor had a 100% success rate, but boy did she drive me hard and to put it quite bluntly I was crammed. Here started my academic problems and I was placed too high in the form lists. Although I was granted a Minor Scholarship which meant only half fees, I got the feeling that in many ways I should not have been there.

But I did go to one of the most famous schools in the world and have never regretted it and I met some great guys there, some of them now quite famous such as Salman Rushdie, who sat beside me for a year. There was also the future commander of HMS Conqueror which sank the Belgrano. And then there were the teachers or beaks. My housemaster had served in the Battle of Britain and enjoyed nothing better in his spare time than translating Gilbert and Sullivan operas into classical Greek – or so I am told. Then there was my German teacher who absolutely hated the Nazis and had served in the Austrian resistance in the war. Not someone to cross swords with by any means, but he could be absolutely charming and on those days he would get his accordion out, we would sing jaunty Tyrolean ditties. My academic record at Rugby was pretty terrible and I only just scraped 5 O levels. I put a lot of work into the A level course but just did not seem to be able to pass exams. But there was the sport and I played a lot of rugby and hockey which was all very enjoyable. I also fenced for the school. Cricket was great fun too and I remember batting in the nets one afternoon and not noticing the Housemaster was perched on his shooting stick directly behind me. I made a ghastly attempt at a cow shot and heard the critical comment from the wicket keeper's position. "Lousy shot Capron." Yes sir was the reply. But I did manage on one occasion to really make a name as a batsman when I hit a six out of the ground. "Good Shot," exclaimed the skipper without actually looking. So, a few shots later I repeated the dose, then I heard the unforgettable comment, "Who was that? Capron? Never!"

There was also the Combined Cadet Force which was taken very seriously, after all there had been six Victoria Crosses awarded to past pupils, including the dreaded Flashman. I amazed the Town House Sergeant by offering to go on the N.C.Os training cadre; he put my name down immediately which meant that I was labelled as a Corps Gut. Never mind, I was granted the rank of Acting Lance Corporal, and by the beginning of the next term the acting bit had dropped off, partly due to a suitably unctuous approach to the Annual Corps Camp. At the end of the term I became a full Corporal and was beginning to think of an Army career. It didn't take long before I moved through the ranks again and took command of both the Town House platoon and the Royal Artillery platoon. I can always say that I have given the order to fire a 25 pounder, even if it was a blank. There certainly was a big bang. There were also the House Platoon Drill Competitions which no house could get out of. I remember parading my platoon and telling them that Town House had been written off so we had nothing to lose and we might as well just give it our best shot! We certainly did and although we did not win we came either second or third, beating some very army oriented houses into the bargain. The Regimental Sergeant Major was highly delighted and sent me a message via my fag that he wanted to see me. At that point, I did not know the results and so with some trepidation, slunk over to the Armoury to find out what I might have done wrong. I had never known the RSM to be so pleased and I soon relaxed to bathe in the verbal sunshine. Although I did look at Sandhurst, in the end, I decided against the armed forces but very nearly went back as a padre some years later.

Fagging was still going on when I was at Rugby and beating still took place in some of the boarding houses, but it was on the way out. My fag is now a senior partner in a firm of Coventry solicitors, I bumped into him the other day and we had a good chat. But time was moving apace and I needed to think about a career and not worry too much about the academic achievements of the high flyers who inevitably led the charge for Oxbridge. What could I do? Academia was certainly not on the drawing board, I had discounted the armed forces, so it was decided that I should attempt a career in banking. At the very least it was respectable. And so I went for interviews at the Local Head Office of Barclays Bank in Birmingham. The powers that be clearly thought that it might be the right thing for both me and them, so in September 1964 I was posted to the Kenilworth branch as the office junior and a glittering career lay ahead of me, or so I thought.

Chapter 3

WORK AND DISCERNING A VOCATION

The days of having one's own fag were soon a distant memory when I started at Barclays, Kenilworth. Sorting cheques for clearing was just one of the mundane jobs that future bank managers had to do, although it was not too long before I learned how to run a till and become the front of house for banking operations. We were warned firmly as to security and to be on guard for robbers. In addition we were told various stories (some apocryphal) of bank raids and the like; such as the visit of the bank inspectors to a remote branch in the outback of Wales. They decided to test the alarm system, and having done so, the door opened and in walked the local pub landlord with a tray of beer. There was also the story of raiders who knew the alarm system at Barclays was situated close to the front door. They pressed the alarm and crossed the road to see the fun. Needless to say, the police turned up, but while they were occupied in their duties, the raiders went down the road and did Lloyds! Little was I to know that in less than two years this would actually happen to me. I enjoyed my time at Kenilworth, even if we had to work on Saturday mornings and there was always a good Chinese lunch to be had opposite the bank for five shillings and an extra sixpence for coffee. New Year's Eve was an interesting experience in those days because the branch had to balance all its books for the previous year. There were horrendous stories of working to midnight, but it wasn't too bad and usually it was the manager, chief clerk and myself who stayed on to complete the work, finishing by 8.00pm at the latest and fortified by a bottle of light ale, courtesy of the manager. I remember on one Christmas Eve, I had an over balance of £60 which was quite a bit of money in those days, in other words I had short changed someone. Fortunately we worked out who it was and we were all able to knock off relatively early.

After some very happy times at Kenilworth, I had my call up papers which told me to report to the Warwick branch. I had clearly moved up a peg and now occupied the Chief Clerk's stool at lunchtime when he went down to the pub for a liquid lunch. It was a complete change, with me learning all about securities, mortgages, legal charges, bills of lading, conveyances, stocks and shares etc. Warwick was a bit old fashioned as they had only just got rid of hand written current accounts and the ledgers were there for all to see, but, there was a sub branch down at Coten End and soon I was asked to run it. We had a good local clientele down there. I had a bank guard who was a Town Councillor and magistrate so the police often popped in to have warrants signed; we reckoned we were very safe. There was the early morning rush of the fish and chip man who paid in his takings suitably mixed with hardened chips and bits of cod. There was also the shoe shop man who came in for a chat and the mini supermarket manager, but most important of all there was the Bookie. He was not a customer of ours, but we had an arrangement whereby we gave him change and in return he allowed me and my bank guard to have a weekly account for our six pence each way bets. The rush being over we settled down to discuss form and then the bets were placed and settlement day was Friday. We never made much and we never lost much, it was just a bit of fun. If we were especially bored then we could always wander over to the gorgeous blonde at Lloyds and change ten shilling notes for one pound notes. Well that was our excuse! It was all very laid back and even the bus drivers would leave their passengers in the bus and cross over the road to pay in some money. Happy days. But every now and again I went back up to the main branch to run the security desk and then one day it happened. They had clearly done their homework, the manager was on holiday and the Chief Clerk being a man of habit was down the pub for lunch. The girls were upstairs in the machine room with the young lad and the chief cashier was at her till. Then they came in. There was a shout and two masked raiders entered wearing stocking masks and holding scaffolder's spanners. One raider protected the door while the other one vaulted over the counter and jumped on me and struck me six times on the head. I then put in one of my scrum half tackles to bring him down. We ended up in a heap on the floor, but unfortunately I was underneath and then the raider turned round and pointed his spanner in my direction. It was at this moment I thought he had a revolver and that I was going to be shot, so I froze. He hesitated and then he saw me press the alarm and realised that it was time to go. The girls upstairs were terrified and fortunately for me, the chief cashier was not hurt and also pressed the alarm with the result that two alarms went off down at the Nick which promptly turned out in force. But there being a one way system at Warwick, the police came down one road and the crooks went up the other. No money was taken, even though there was £20K in the safe. There was a lot of my blood about the place, in fact it looked like a butcher's shop. They never got the raiders, but I never forgot that day. There was one good thing about it and that was that all my old girlfriends came round to see me!

After some further time at Barclays I began to find banking to be very boring and respectable, so I thought I would take the opportunity to go out to Switzerland and work there with all sorts of opportunities for travel. I had only been in Neuchatel for about four months when it became apparent that Switzerland was not for me, although my command of the French language became very good. I returned home and signed on the dole, but it was only a few weeks after that I was offered a job as a Builder's mate for £2 per day and free beer on pay day down at the Conservative Club. However something was beginning to stir and I found myself thinking more and more about the possibility of the ordained ministry.

Trying to rack my brains as to when this all started and whether there had been a low key Damascus Road experience, I homed in on Rugby School, which despite its rather watery Public School religion had actually provided the spark. I recalled an assistant school chaplain who was a bit on the High Church side. What I liked about him was that he was ordinary and not wallowing in academic self righteousness. To my mind, even in those early days, he was a priest and I was always made very welcome at his house where his delightful wife was constantly serving hot buttered toast to hungry schoolboys. In addition there were one or two other priests at Rugby, one of whom, Jack MacDonough used to celebrate Holy Communion most faithfully on every Saints day and Holy Day as prescribed by the Church of England. That faithfulness made a big impression on me and I had the added bonus of actually boarding with Jack for close on two years when my father was appointed Chief Fire Officer and had to move to Leamington Spa. Jack was Irish and had played hockey for his country; he was certainly quite a character.

To return to my working life. I had started to go to church at St. Mary Magdalene, Lillington, but it was not on a regular basis as there was much more to do which was interesting. The new vicar turned up who happened also to be an Old Rugbeian. This seemed a good opportunity to make friends, so one evening I decided to afford the Almighty an hour of my valuable time, put on my old boys' tie and went to Evensong. Joe Humble saw the tie, came over to me and said that I must join him next Sunday at Rugby because he was the guest preacher and there was a free lunch going with the new Headmaster. It was good to go back, but it didn't take long before Joe told me that he needed some new altar servers and I was just the ticket. Soon I was wearing robes and kneeling piously at the altar. Then I was elected to the PCC, then the Deanery Synod, Council of Churches, Assistant Choirmaster etc. I had the bug and to make matters more interesting there were some very attractive girl servers called serviettes.

I need to digress away from the church for a moment and look at the great game of Rugby Football, which was my other love. It did not take too long before I fell in with the lads of Whitnash RFC. We used to play on the ground belonging to the Sports and Social Club, but following a row with the committee we walked out and set up shop at Harbury. I was soon on the committee; vice captain of the seconds and enjoying myself in the scrum half position. I got myself into the first XV and finished up as Club Captain as well as Secretary of the South Warwickshire Union. Nevertheless the stirring was still there and some of my rugby friends noticed that I was no longer leading the singing and tending to sit away from the fun. When I told them that I was going into the church after a particularly hard game away to Banbury 3rd XV, there was much merriment and I was anointed with beer, dirty water and anything else that came to hand. I had had a good game, specialising in taking out the opposing winger with flying tackles, so I remember the occasion well. What was interesting was that a bet was made by the President that I would not be ordained. The Chairman who had been an altar server disagreed and accepted the bet of £5 which he collected on the steps of Coventry Cathedral when I was ordained. There is more to come on my rugby activities later, but Harbury RFC came en bloc to my ordination and it was great to see them there. I thoroughly enjoyed going to their 40 year anniversary and I am looking forward to the fiftieth next year. I will have had some connection with them for close on 47 years. No regrets at all and so many stories to tell.

And now another digression. This time into the world of loss adjusting. It didn't take too long for my parents to get a bit fed up with me walking up Cloister Way from my labouring job. For one thing, I looked grotty and for another, the job prospects were not exactly rosy. Eventually I ended up looking for another career, this time in the business of settling insurance claims and although the Church was now well and truly established at the back of my mind, I was ready to broaden my outlook which is something that the church authorities are always going on about.

I served in Birmingham, Northampton and Coventry. The job of a Loss Adjuster is to investigate the cause of the loss; to check whether it is covered under the terms of the insurance policy and then to negotiate a settlement. That all sounds quite straightforward, but people are not straightforward and when they think that the Insurance Company is going to take money off them, by not paying the full amount, then amazingly they become awkward. Throw in for good measure having to deal with some of the Del Boy characters who controlled the salvage market and it all becomes quite interesting.

I well remember going out on a claim which was clearly fraudulent. The claimant knew that and so did I and the claimant knew that I knew. It ended up with an attack on the claimant by outsiders in a cafe, with furniture flying around in all directions and me sheltering under a table. I managed to get out and arrived back in the office to much mirth. On another occasion, I happened to be in a bedroom, measuring up walls for water damage when it was quite obvious to me that I was walking into a trap because the woman started to take off her clothes! I got out double quick. But it was the claim in South Birmingham which involved the total destruction by fire of a lounge and all its contents that finally settled my thoughts on the matter of ordination. The claimant was an agent for Avon cosmetics and the lounge was where she met her customers. It was well appointed and she was clearly proud of it, but she had a drunken husband who spent most of his time with other women and he wanted lots of cash. I explained the terms of the policy and that it only provided for an indemnity, in other words, I had to make allowances for improvement and the claimant could not expect to receive new lamps for old. The building claim was easy to settle, but the contents claim was going to be the sticking point. I explained that she must make due allowance in her claim for the fact that many of the contents were a few years old. She did not get the message and when the claim came into the office it totalled about £500. I took the claim to my boss who said quite bluntly that I should offer her £180 and not to come back into the office having paid more than £200. I was told to get out and settle. She burst into tears telling me that her husband would beat her. He was behind the door listening so that was a definite possibility. I stuck to my guns and eventually settled at £200. I returned to the office feeling absolutely ghastly and it was then that the overall boss said to me, "David, I think you should be a priest!"

I soon left loss adjusting and worked as a dustman in Leamington Spa. It was the best money that I had ever earned and my mate was a lively lad called, "Fingers" who had done porridge for a GBH job. I got on with him fine and he was well liked by the old folk, he just had a problem with authority. And so say all of us. That was the last time that I earned money in the real world because I was moving rapidly towards Theological College. Now I want to go back a few years and tell the story of how I actually got there.

Clearly other people had begun thinking that I might go into the Church. There were two assistant curates at Lillington who were both first class and came from opposite ends of the liturgical candle. They had both been well trained in their respective traditions. Stephen Tyrrell who came from the evangelical stable, lived with his family in a council house up on the estate and did great work with a massive Sunday School. David McCormack from the more catholic end lived in a curate's house at the other end of the parish where you could stretch your arm through the brickwork from the outside, into the living room. He tended to look after the Church Youth Club and matters sacramental. Both curates had obviously discussed the matter and so it was after Evensong when David beckoned me over and said that he wanted to have a word. I now needed to speak to the Vicar and Joe Humble packed me off to see the Diocesan Director of Ordination. However, before that first meeting it had been suggested by both Stephen and David that I should go and make a retreat. I decided to go to Kelham Monastery, which was an Anglican foundation and also trained young men for the ordained ministry. It was a ghastly journey and the weather was foul. Mind you the food was even worse and to compound matters, the retreat was in total silence. Nobody had told me! What stood out for me was that amazing chapel with the brick built arch stretching from one side to the other. Yes I could smell incense, and plenty of it, but I could sense holiness and powerful witness. It was St. Luke's tide and I made a note to have a moan at the curates when I returned for having failed to warn me about total silence.

My first meeting with the DDO was a bit awkward as I think we were trying to get to know one another. Father Mark Meynell was incumbent of Leamington Hastings and although living in some style, clearly practised Christian humility. He was holiness incarnate and I came away, feeling that I had been in the company of a modern day saint. Further meetings ensued and I remember him teaching me about the seven sacraments and also that I needed at sometime to make my confession, which incidentally did not take place for about another four years. He told me that he would admit me to the Diocesan Fellowship of Vocation at the next meeting, but when I arrived, he clearly had had second thoughts and said that I was not quite ready. I went away with a heavy heart and next day went to the lunchtime Eucharist at Holy Trinity, Coventry which was just down the road from the Loss Adjusters office. I had a quick chat with the officiating priest, Father Stephen Pedley and must have mentioned my concerns about the Fellowship of Vocation. The next thing that happened was an invitation to be altar server with lunch at the Alhambra (a local hostelry) afterwards, where, I was assured, the Guinness came direct from Dublin! Stephen was the ideal person to cheer me up and I was soon back on track. His ministry was to be wide and varied: missionary work in Zambia, parish priest in two incumbencies in Durham Diocese, Canon Residentiary, Chaplain to the Queen and finally Suffragan Bishop of Lancaster. I owe him a lot and when I was serving in Durham Diocese, he was my confessor. He was the son of a Coventry priest and his wife Mary was also parsonage bred. We keep in touch to this day and I have a parishioner in Alcester who used to worship with him in the northeast.

Eventually, the diocesan authorities decided that I should go to a selection conference, but I still needed to be sponsored and checked over by a Bishop. It was my good fortune to be interviewed by Bishop John Mackie, a delightful Australian who wanted nothing more than to talk about rugby, football and cricket. It was with much regret that for the last five minutes we really got down to discuss matters of an ecclesiastical bent. So, after much form filling and reference taking, I was informed that I should present myself in Cheltenham at what I think was termed a diocesan retreat centre, together with about twenty other candidates where we would undergo spiritual, academic and personality assessment. We would be set various tasks to perform with feedback to a plenary session, having to lead discussions, and there was a session with the selection secretary dealing with more mundane matters such as finance. To make matters worse, we learned that the demolition contractors were moving in, once we had finished.

The selectors looked pretty fearsome; however the Conference Chairman was the Archdeacon of Canterbury who liked nothing better than to talk about cricket. He really was a delightful and very spiritual person. I must confess that I did rather enjoy myself and felt that if it was to be, then so be it. What happened was that after we had left, the selectors gathered together and looked at each candidate. There were three main classifications; (a) a straightforward recommendation, (b) a negative decision, but with encouragement to come back again and (c) don't phone us, we will phone you. In addition there was a possible modification of (a), whereby you might be asked to go out into the world for a year. Clearly that would not apply in my case. At the end of the day it was only a recommendation and bishops did not have to accept the advice, inevitably they did, and in any case there was always the implied threat that head office held the purse strings. Very few bishops broke rank.

I gathered later that the academic selector found me difficult to work out, but in fairness to him he realised that I had a big problem in passing exams, so he felt that a three year course for me should not include exams, but just essays. So I waited and waited. We had set up a matrix of contact numbers so that we could find out how our recently made friends had made out. I had a straightforward recommendation, but, that the Theological College should put me on the essay course. Unfortunately for me, paperwork was lost and I eventually went straight onto an exam course. As far as my friends were concerned, some of us met up at college, others were accepted and went elsewhere. One or two were turned down flat; the selectors soon sniffed them out. One or two needed to come back again.

So, it was off to select a college, having first of all undergone a medical examination. I had set my heart on Wells and was offered a place much to my delight. Westcott House was booked up for a couple of years and so I looked at Cuddesdon in Oxford. It was far too academic for me and a bit on the pious side, so I said no to that. Hence I prepared to live in my home county for the first time since 1948 and then came the shock – Wells was to close. There was one year left, so I decided that I would still go and then go to Salisbury afterwards.

Chapter 4

WELLS

My time at Wells was the best year of my life. It was good to be living in my home county and the environment was wonderful. Wells was basically a combination of a public school and a country club, so clearly I was going to enjoy myself. Having said that, the academic work was relentless and you had to keep your head down. Morning Prayer started at 7.15am in the undercroft of the cathedral, followed by Holy Eucharist. Morning Prayer was compulsory, but you could nip out after the morning office if you wanted. If I remember rightly, evening prayer was about 6.00pm and you were expected to spend 30 minutes of solitude somewhere in the cathedral beforehand. On Monday morning you were expected to maintain silence until lunchtime, which meant that breakfast was also silent.

There were three new entrants that term, myself, Geoff and Henry. Geoff lived with his wife and father a little bit out of town and Henry, being like me a single man, lived in college, which for most of us meant Vicars Close. To live in a 14th C. street was out of this world and perhaps this caused a somewhat detached view of the church. Very few parishes, even in the most top notch area could boast a scenario like that. Not much raw life there, but a wonderful place to study and undergo priestly formation.

We lived in houses of about six ordinands with a resident cook and steward. Meals were very much a family affair and the lecturers sat in from time to time. We all had domestic duties to perform, coupled with odd jobs around the college and, of course there was the conduct of worship. It did not take long before I was dragged in to act as an acolyte wearing, alb, amice, apparel etc and carrying candles. There was also Sunday duty, which was a doddle for me, because when it was established that I played the organ, it so happened that I was granted a series of lessons on the cathedral organ at a big discount, for which I played once per week up at a small Mendip Chapel. The chapel had a regular congregation of three, presided over by a very elderly lady who had been baptised, confirmed, married there and was going to be taken out of there in her coffin! On the one occasion the Bishop of Bath and Wells came, he soon knew his place. I preached my first sermon there and the visiting priest went through the sermon over a pint of beer in the pub afterwards. I then went up to Bristol for the night with my pal (also ordained in later life) and a couple of girls.

But to get back to the daily offices. You were expected to be properly attired and to start on time. God help you if you did not. The cathedral bell rang and you rose from the desk to start. Even if you were a very few seconds late, the Principal would comment loudly in chapel, "Is there a problem?"

I was introduced to spontaneous prayer which was quite novel for me. Anything could happen and invariably did. "Lord, we pray for those who do not like us, especially the Dean and Chapter" – unfortunately, the Canon Precentor was lurking in the vestry and heard it all. The college lost a few Brownie house points for that. Then there were those with political points to score. On one occasion at the time of the Rhodesia crisis, there was a Rhodesian ordinand and when some ordinands prayed that Ian Smith might see sense and end his rebellion, they got more than they prayerfully thought was their due.

The college was basically, "radical catholic" with a strong minority of evangelicals who were more than prepared to fight their corner! Biblical study was rigorous and I soon began to see the old testament in a totally different light. I learned about biblical criticism and also how to analyse the synoptic gospels. Then there was doctrine which I found very difficult and basically struggled with it for much of my time. Liturgy and Church History, I thoroughly enjoyed, also spirituality.

Perhaps the most enjoyable service of the week was Compline in the ancient chapel at the top of Vicars Close. It was sung in Gregorian chant which was beautiful and also a good way to round off the week on Fridays. Needless to say, I invariably found myself making for the Fountain Inn which was just outside of the Cathedral Liberty. Imagine my delight when I was told that countless ordinands had made it their watering hole over the years, including some very famous personages. But best of all, it was the headquarters of Wells RFC and it did not take long for me to join up and begin playing regularly again.

I used to go up with the secretary Bob Green on a Saturday morning to the Bath and West Showground where the matches were played. We started off by shifting some of the sheep, then checking if the ferrets were

OK, then picking up the cow pats and throwing them into the hedgerow and finally ensuring that the hot water system in the stockmen's cubicles actually worked. There was just about enough to fill one metal bath and that had to be enough for 30 players plus the ref. Talking of refs we had our favourite who was a Fleet Chief from R.N.A.S. Yeovilton. He did not take any messing, he knew the rules, he was fair, he joined in the singing in the bar and he bought his round. Needless to say, he was always welcome. Wells RFC consisted of a lot of the boys in blue, the station sergeant was skipper and the inspector led the pack. It was always said that if you wanted to raid a bank in Wells, then Saturday was the best day to do it. Another skipper was called Bill Bishop and he was a very big christian in all senses of the word and very much into mission. On one occasion he came lumbering up beside me when I was making a break for the line and in a west country accent was heard to say, "Come on Vicar, pass the ball" to which my reply was, "Certainly Bishop".

But to go back to college life. There were special days such as Ascension day when we went up onto the roof of the Chapter House to sing hymns and then there was a party in the evening with entertainment. Somehow or other I found myself being the MC and also the bar steward. We dined in the Lay Vicars banqueting hall which lay upstairs and between the cathedral and Vicars Close. Pewter mugs and plates were the order of the day. I ordered too much beer, so for about one week I was running a highly illegal bar from the cellar of one of the houses. I had good company because the lecturers used to join us before lunch and fortunately for me there was no complaint and I managed to balance the books.

College Council or "Koinonia" was always great fun where students and staff could get to grips with some thorny social problems. The bookshop was run by the students who looked after most things which had a touch of commerce linked to them. The college had a good portion of older students and many of them had been in business, so such enterprises as mentioned were in very good hands.

Relations with the local community were very good and needless to say many a local girl had become a vicar's wife. We had an annual visit to the magistrate's court where we were virtually bowed in by a butler. The Chairman of the bench was the local undertaker supported by the local butcher etc. It was great and the JPs were very courteous to the accused. One of the main problems around Wells was that of incest, although on the day we attended, there was no relevant case waiting for trial. The chairman was very efficient but he had a hard side to him and had hit the Sunday papers for sending a man to prison for nicking one bottle of milk! Mind you, he already had a suspended sentence. We also had first rate relations with the local RCs. When it came to the daily Angelus, the cathedral got in first with its bells but the local RC priest had always known in the past where to get a good meal. He used to celebrate mass at 8.00am and then go up to the Anglican Theological College for a cooked breakfast. After that he took the Anglican ordinands with him up to Downside Abbey where they used to engage in Beagling. Very much a country pursuit. Perhaps that is why the college just had to close. Or perhaps it was because the staff were often firing off letters of a critical nature to the Church Times which did not make them popular.

The cathedral services were done according to the liturgical book and were most impressive, especially Choral Evensong which was sung to a very high standard. Then there was the Sung Eucharist on Sunday morning with full vestments which was even more impressive when Jock Henderson the Bishop was presiding. He was a Prince of the Church and was always absolutely charming and courteous, it did not matter who he was talking to, and when he processed into church, the worshippers bowed like willows in the wind. He had style, but he had also been around. He had served as a padre in the Royal Navy in the war and obviously had a few important connections. So when Princess Margaret wanted some space after the Townsend affair, then it was to Wells and the Bishop's Palace that she went. And yet, Jock Henderson was also a very normal man. One of his favourite pursuits was to take off his episcopal gear and change into old and dirty clothes, when he would cross over moat and walk down the back street so that he could go and drink cider with his workers. When he gave a party, he sure gave a party. There was a tradition that he always entertained the new intake in the palace. We all wondered whether he would do it for the final year, but we need not have feared. The invitations came and we reported to the palace for a personally guided tour. I noticed a signed photograph of Princess Margaret on his desk and then came the drinks and the food. He had shipped in the diocesan staff who were busily dispensing substantial quantities of best quality local cider. I must admit that I do not remember all that much of the party, but at least I could honestly say that I had been with the Bishop.

There was another party that I had not been invited to, but the college organist had, with the result that next morning we were told that his wife was not allowing him out, and that I had to play the organ for the cathedral Sung Eucharist. I protested, but was told that I could not get out of it as it was the turn of the college to cover the service, thus giving the canons and the choir a Sunday off. With a very heavy heart, I climbed the stairs to the organ loft and hesitatingly pulled out a few stops. I did have some basic Bach which might do for the introit and exeunt, but there were the hymns and also the setting. It was just a few minutes to go and I was about to have a heart attack when I heard a gentle stepping noise and the college organist appeared by my side, looking a little pale. I will not repeat what I said to him as it was of a somewhat unchristian nature, but he took over and I quickly slipped down the stairs to go and worship with everyone else.

We also went to the parish church of St. Cuthbert each term and that was a very interesting experience as there was a very canny old priest there called Father Mack. We were very fond of him as he did not mince his words and did not suffer fools gladly. How refreshing we thought, why does not the Church of England do this more often? I remember one service which included the sacrament of baptism. Father Mack got up in the pulpit to preach, as he did so he looked somewhat suspiciously at the congregation and then quite deliberately spoke as follows, "In a few minutes, some of you (parents and godparents) are going to make some solemn and binding promises and in a few days most of you will have committed perjury." Mind you he was absolutely right, but he did have his detractors. It was also good to worship at an ordinary parish church without the all consuming presence of the cathedral. We always looked forward to our visit to St. Cuthbert's.

By now time was running out for Wells and those of us who were going to make the trip to Salisbury were not completely happy. Nevertheless we challenged Salisbury to a cricket match, which on the face of it we should not have had a chance with our 17 ordinands and approaching 100 at Salisbury. Still, we had a secret weapon which was that two of our players had played at a high level and one of them was mentioned in Wisden, and so, what with our own umpire who had operated at minor counties level, we absolutely massacred them. It was a triumphant evening Eucharist that day and even the sermon was suitably complimentary. Needless to say, we had to go over and have a look at Salisbury, which even I found to be too

High Church – believe it or not. It seemed to be a little precious and I did find the 'camp' element to be a little disturbing in the early days; however I would be the first to say that many of the guys have turned out to be first rate priests; loving and faithful to their flocks. I also remember a T. Group session which was all about group dynamics. It was not handled very well and in the end most of us from Wells went off down the local pub and formed our group down there.

So we were almost at the last gate now. Those who were to be ordained that Petertide had already got their title parishes sorted out and had printed their own ordination prayer cards. Arrangements were being made to move the library over to Salisbury which incidentally contained an original version of Calvin's Institutions. The last day and the last service came that much nearer by the hour. Dinings out, last drinks, last Koinonia, last Sunday morning gathering and that session which was called, "Apologetics!" And then it happened and the tears began to run under the undercroft door. It was absolutely ghastly. I was dumbfounded because Wells meant so much to me; I had even passed my exams. The final hymn was a good old fashioned one called, "What a friend we have in Jesus" and I played it on the organ. So a radical catholic college went out with an evangelical flourish. Not bad really, because both traditions are very christo-centric. So I went back home and worked as an acting, unpaid and un-ordained curate to Bishop John Daly who was Vicar of Bishops Tachbrook, having been formerly Bishop of Korea. It was one of the best things I ever did, because a few years later, it was to be my saving grace. Irrespective of that, I really had a great time with the old boy. I got to work on parish charities and met a very young David Dumbleton, the future Diocesan Registrar, who for my money has been one of the best servants that any diocese could possibly ask for. I took school assemblies, led choir practice, preached and attended formal parish meetings. It was the best training that any ordinand could get. Then one day, BJ (as he was known), asked if I could drop him at the cathedral and pick him up later. That was no problem, and when I returned to the cathedral, he breezily told me that he just married my bishop! I don't think many people knew about the relationship of Bishop Cuthbert and Miss Mitchell from Alveston. Not many people could have taken on Cuthbert, but he was a great, great bishop.

Chapter 5

SALISBURY

On arrival at my new college in Salisbury, I could see the cathedral with a superb spire and a delightful close which had its own police force. At night the gates are locked and there are many stories of ordinands being locked out and having to get back in via the wall at the back of the pub! Salisbury is an interesting city, although very different to Wells and has some glorious countryside. I used to go down to chapel each morning from the convent and enter the close by a smaller gate on the south side. The Morning Offices and Eucharists were reasonably similar to Wells and there was an additional chapel which had been designed by Butterfield, who of course had designed the chapel at Rugby School. I still went back to Wells at weekends to play rugby and see old friends, which kept me sane. However, I seemed to manage academically and engaged in a few additional activities such as teaching the occasional lesson at the grammar school in the Close and also refereeing the odd rugby match at the Cathedral School. I was attached to the Bemerton group so that I and others could hone our pastoral skills. This was George Herbert country of course and we all took it in turns to preach and lead ordinary parish church services: the vicar, Max Williams, was very supportive and used to come into college for a drink from time to time. By an amazing stroke of good luck, it transpired when I was in Alcester that the local Baptist minister and he were brothers.

It had been decided by the student body that a bar should be set up in college: no prizes for guessing who volunteered to run it. At least I had my pal Geoff on board for that and we set to work with a vengeance. However it did not start off too well, because we needed to apply for a licence and there were clearly objections from some of the matrons in the close who thought that their impressionable young daughters might be shocked at seeing bare chested draymen and hearing their robust language. The application was turned down, so we tried again and found unlikely support from the college bursar who had recently come out of the army and rather liked the idea of a gin and tonic before going home. He put up another application notice on the college gate pillar and *unfortunately* allowed the ivy to fall down and cover it over. What a shame! The application was approved. So the great day arrived and it seemed appropriate to invite Harold Wilson – yes, that was the name of the College Principal, to perform the opening ceremony. I must confess that he was in good form and a very convivial time was had by all. Bass Light was on sale at 14p per pint, Carling Black Label at 16p per pint and Newcastle Brown was offered at 16p per bottle. We also sold plenty of gin and, (once we had been advised by our Bahamian ordinands), plenty of quality rum. It did not take long for the girls at the teacher training college in the Close to hear about it and soon Friday night was quite a night. I would take about £100 on those evenings! Incidentally there are some very senior members of the Church of England now getting towards the end of their ministry who were particularly good customers of mine. No names mentioned of course.

An interesting deviation from normality was the six weeks placement at the Elephant and Castle in London. I must confess that I thoroughly enjoyed myself, perhaps in all fairness because I was away from college. I was attached to the South London Industrial Mission which was interesting to say the least. In many ways they were quite prophetic and would have been laughed out of court in normal times, but although I did not always agree with them, that placement did help me when I went up northeast and was involved with the Teeside Industrial Mission. We also did parish visiting and attended a few ecumenical sessions. On one occasion we asked if we could liven up worship a bit on the visit of the Bishop of Woolwich who at that time was David Shepherd. We made a merry noise that night with drums and cymbals joining in. We also enjoyed the company of the Vicar (Keith Pound) who went on to become Chaplain General to the Prison Service, it was a very good idea of his to take us out for a pub crawl on our first Sunday – after evensong of course!

It was then back to college and the prospect of exams started to loom. Without appearing to be melodramatic, I think I made the mistake that Newman made all those years ago, by over revising. That may well be the nearest that I shall ever get to sainthood, but it didn't do me any good, especially as I was working for 12 hours every day. To cut a long story short, I failed the lot and so they put me belatedly on an essay scheme and I failed that. There was nothing for it but to go home and lick my wounds and count the cost. So I returned to worried parents and the need to work for a while and see whether the powers that be might let me go back and finish off. I then went down with stress and was signed off anyway. So I engaged in voluntary ministry once again with my old friend BJ. It was about this time that my parents went off to Kenya for a safari holiday and I thought that I would drive down to Heathrow to pick them up. It was very early morning when I arrived, probably about 2.00am. Then, something stirred within me which told me that I had some unfinished business with the Almighty. Fortunately for me there was a chapel at the airport. I well remember it because it was underground and very cavernous. So I went down there and got on my knees. After a while I knew what I had to do, and it actually meant letting go of myself and handing myself over to God and saying basically, over to you! I stretched out my hands in the sign of the cross, just like the Franciscans do to this day at Cross Prayers; I paused for a while and then went back upstairs to meet my parents.

Well, in many ways things went on as per normal but I did get a temporary job at the General Accident Insurance branch in Coventry, back to my old trade of insurance claims, however it was only temporary and I was soon back with BJ. And then something happened. The old boy felt that he could not stand back any longer and do nothing so when writing a letter to his old friend Bishop Cuthbert on a totally unrelated subject, he finished off by saying that David Capron wished to be remembered to him and was hoping to get back to college A.S.A.P. The next morning the phone rang and BJ came in to see me saying that "the boss" wanted words with me. "I am covered in dust and ashes," said Cuthbert, "do come and see me." "When?" I asked, "Tomorrow" was the reply. So the next day I was ushered into the Presence to be greeted by the great man who immediately said that he wanted to see me in Coventry Cathedral in June. "What for?" I said. "I am going to ordain you," was the reply. "But what about Head Office in London?" I protested, to hear those immortal words of authority, "I am the Bishop, I make these decisions, not London, and I will sort out the money, now," and he paused, "I want you to go and see Father Anthony Rowe at St. Mary Magdalen, Hearsall Common, he needs a new curate." And it was all signed and sealed, just like that. What some of you would not know is that my file had been lost and I did not exist. The diocese made up for this by inviting me to read the gospel at the ordination service, which was a great honour and shook my parents.

I had a second chat with Bishop Cuthbert and he asked what I needed to top up with at college and we agreed that moral theology needed a second look, but above all, just getting back into the rhythm of priestly life. I somewhat cheekily said that I would take over the bar again as it had fallen on hard times. "What a good idea," said Cuthbert and, as I am sure you will all agree, it is always a good idea to have the approval of your bishop.

So it was back to college where I had a very warm welcome and, there had been a change of principal. I enjoyed those last two terms and topped up on my moral theology, taking care to attend as many lectures as I could fit in on a voluntary basis covering all aspects of theology. I looked after the bar again, but the prices had gone up! Never mind, I would soon be able to celebrate properly.

There were one or two other matters to attend to, especially as it was all taking place in a bit of a hurry. Firstly, I needed to sort out clerical and liturgical wear, which necessitated a trip to London. Having obtained the permission of the new principal, I made for Thomas Pratt and Son of Covent Garden. It was just like stepping back into Dickensian mode. There was a wooden desk with what looked like a quill pen in position and a very elderly gentleman who rose to enquire if he could possibly be of assistance. He was Mr. Pratt and there were three other partners in the business, Mr. Pratt, Mr. Pratt and Mr. Pratt! I obtained all that I needed, having first established that the liturgical colour for ordination would be white. This was very much in my line of thinking as representing Christian Initiation. Unfortunately today, the Holy Spirit has intruded, so the ordination colour tends to be red. Anyway, I digress, so back to college I went and started to get to know the new principal. He was a Wells man, through and through which meant that in my eyes, he could do no wrong. He had a superb command of the Queens' English, admittedly, a little rustic at times with just hints of rural innuendo. There has only been one person in my life who bettered him and that was my headmaster at Rugby, Dr. Walter Hamilton, and only one person who got anywhere near him and that was my curate in Newton Aycliffe, Reverend Doctor Frank Colman.

We were getting towards the end of term and the big and final service of Forthgoing, but I did need to pop back to Wells and see some old friends again. I remember checking out the bar cellar and doing a proper stock check. When I returned, I repeated the exercise because the bar had been open and got a big shock because I was a crate of Newcastle Brown short and crate of red wine short. I had a sleepless night and went back down again after Morning Prayer. The results were the same. What had happened? Then all was revealed as Reggie, the new Principal came mooching down the corridor. "Ah, my dear David," he said, "I was meaning to tell you that I had a dinner party last night and as I knew where the key was I helped myself, meaning of course to square up with you at the earliest opportunity." What I said was rather different to what I thought of saying. I just suggested that next time he had a dinner party he ask me first and I would be very happy to give him my complete and undivided attention. "That is very good of you my dear David," he said rather mysteriously and glided away. You live and learn!

Prayer cards were my next concern and I was able to place an order with the Poor Clares at Freeland. I made a point of sending one to each church with which I had had connections in the past and received some very interesting replies. Then it was almost upon us and the Forthgoing Service was ready to start. The tradition had been for those ordinands who were being sent out to sit together as a recognised body. I do not remember much of the service, but I do remember the Forthgoing which took place during the singing of, "Thine be the glory." As the chorus started with the words, "rolled the stone away", we got up and went out for the last time. I have always found that hymn to be very moving and it brings out a little of the charismatic from within me. Then it was down to the bar to find that, horror of horrors the new bar staff had not ordered enough beer, let alone gin, so I had to make just one more phone call in that respect.

Next morning it was homewards and making preparations for my own retreat which led me into the formal diocesan retreat at Alveston Leys a few days later. It was great there, tea in bed and croquet on the lawn plus a dramatic ordination charge from Bishop Cuthbert. Having had a little trouble with putting on my clerical collar for the first time, I was a little stressed when we eventually drove off to Coventry Cathedral for the big service and just a few pounds in money terms, lighter. We had to pay for our retreat.

Chapter 6

ORDINATION AND TITLE CURACY

I was ordained Deacon by Bishop Michael Parker on June 29th 1975, the Feast of St. Peter, Apostle and Martyr. Bishop Michael had retired to the diocese having been Bishop of Bradford. The Priests were ordained by Bishop John Mackie, and the reason Bishop Cuthbert did not preside was that the Queen was at Stratford upon Avon and he was duty bound to be present. We transacted legal business beforehand and then processed into a packed cathedral behind Archdeacon Ted Taylor, who, having served in the army, said in a militaristic tone, "Forward men". If you get a chance, next time in the cathedral, see if you can spot the coins set into the floor so that the procession can be properly spaced out? Well the service proceeded apace and I could see my parents and the entire membership of Harbury R.F.C. plus some other relatives. Then came the gospel, and I was verged into position. It went amazingly well and the Precentor, (Howard Poole), shook hands with me and said, "Well read". Praise indeed from someone who was to be referred to as Rentaprecentor. About a week later I sent off a letter of thanks to him, especially for arranging for my mother who was blind to have a good seat and, also for looking after the Rugby Club! I received a reply by return. "Dear Mr Capron, thank you for your letter, that is the first time in my life that anyone has written to me to thank me for organising an ordination, do phone my secretary and come over to take a glass of sherry." Clearly, I was now, well and truly in the Church. There was also another incident just after the service, when we were all carted off to a side chapel for some further and final ecclesiastical business conducted by the ever youthful David Dumbleton. He commenced the meeting with the immortal words, "Reverend Gentlemen". I was in.

But to get back to the parish; I needed to be introduced and, as I was told later, the arrival of a new, and relatively young curate who was single, certainly gave them something to talk about. I had been warned that a previous curate had fallen for one of the girls in the youth club, and the previous vicar had married the daughter of his landlady. It certainly did not do him any harm as he went on to become Dean of Hereford. So, the marriage brokers were on full alert.

The parish of St. Mary Magdalen, Hearsall Lane was known as having the church with the blue roof. It sat close to Hearsall Common and had grown up with the local Baptist and Roman Catholic communities. It had been extremely "High" in its day and I saw a picture of a procession close to the RCs with incense, biretta, cope, acolytes etc; all the gear, and they were the local Anglicans. Things had died down a bit and although the church was on the high side it was now much more mainstream. Hearsall/Chapelfields was the area where the watch makers set up shop. It was inhabited by craftsmen, although some had by now moved out. They were very precise, as you would expect, and this precision sometimes caused problems. Because they had all been craftsmen and because the tram had come to the bottom of the road, the area was considered to be upper working class. They did not have much time for Earlsdon, which was next door and considered them to be a load of snobs. Earlsdon was a middle class area (lower), because the tram actually came up the middle of the road, rather than just stopping at the bottom.

Father Anthony Rowe was my training vicar and I have to say, that he could not be bettered, as well as being a safe pair of hands. He did not believe in staff meetings, because we met every day for Morning Prayer, mass and evening prayer, so if anything needed to be discussed, it could be dealt with then. I read myself in at evensong on ordination day and then signed yet another form. There then followed the inevitable bun fight when they could see what I really looked like. The next morning, the boss gave me a list of 40 parishioners to visit in my first week, to be followed by even more. I soon learned that on parish visiting, you need to keep going and not to spend too long at one address, as the parishioners would have compared notes anyway. I was also very keen to show my loyalty and if there were any grumbles, then I duly reported back. I understood that as a deacon, I was only expected to preach once per month and so the great day arrived and I glided into the pulpit, the boss having given advance warning so that there could be a full house. I understood that my predecessor had been known to preach for a fairly long time and so, fortified with that knowledge, the organist slid off his stool and slunk off to the toilet where he could sit down and enjoy a long cigarette. Unfortunately, I did my usual short job, finishing with the usual turn off, "in the name of the Father and of the Son, and of the Holy Ghost, Amen!" The boss smiled and announced the next hymn; there was total silence. The boss announced it again and then there was the patter of feet as one of the churchwardens sprinted down the side aisle and shot up the stairs to bang on the toilet door! Fortunately, serenity returned and the service finished in the normal manner. At least there were enough complimentary remarks for me to feel reasonably satisfied. Just as a pointer to a later chapter, you will learn that first sermons tended to cause all sorts of problems, but that is for later.

I had moved into a small terraced house only about a hundred yards from the church. There was no phone, (curates don't need phones), so when the boss went away he had to make special arrangements for the undertakers to contact me. You will never believe this, but the undertakers were told to phone the local butcher, who would walk down to my house with the message, I then took the keys to the vicarage, let myself in and phoned back. I got my first funeral earlier than I had expected. I remember it well. The deceased, was the steward of the working men's club down the road and had died on holiday in Malta. I could not make a visit as there were no family around, so all I could do was to turn up at Canley Crematorium very early for the service and speak to some of the Club members outside. To make matters worse, I had picked up a bug which entailed me having to visit the little room at very frequent intervals and so I was not looking my best when the cortege arrived. I did manage to have a quick word with the widow and then we were into the service and fairly soon afterwards we were making our way to the grave. It was then that I noticed with horror that it was one almighty big coffin, so I muttered to Gordon Grimmett the undertaker as to whether he had got his measurements correct. "I do hope so, sir" he said, somewhat pessimistically. I thought to myself, I don't believe this, it is my very first funeral and the coffin will probably not go down the hole! We all gathered around the grave and I gave the order to lower, coupled with a quick prayer for deliverance. Well, they had to tip it length way on and to wriggle it sideways and very grudgingly it went down sufficiently far enough for me to pronounce the words of committal. But that wasn't all, because I had to go back and take another funeral, this time in church and then back for cremation. I was still in some discomfort and to compound the whole rotten day, the organist did not just play the wrong hymn tune he played the wrong metre with the result that it was totally unsingable. What a rotten day, but I was soon well again and enjoying myself. The boss clearly had confidence in me and left me to run the parish while he was on holiday. Needless to say as I was only in deacons orders, I was not able to celebrate the holy mysteries, but there were always priests around who were only too happy to oblige. I had been warned by the boss, that I might need to face up to some of the altar servers who rather liked overusing the incense! Not everyone liked incense in the parish, yet there were enough to justify its use on Sundays, so I was determined that it would not take over and that there would be some element of control. On the first Sunday, I stamped my authority and barred them from taking the incense boat with them around the church in the procession, which meant that they could not top up the thurible and make even more smoke. I insisted that the incense boat be left on the altar rails where everyone could see it. There were mutters, but I won that fight.

Believe it or not, I actually moved house within six months of arriving. An old priest, (Father Oliver) had died in the parish and had left his house to the PCC. It was even closer than the vicarage to the church and so it was suggested that I might like to move at the expense of the PCC, which would save the rent. This I did, moving from No. 77, Sir Thomas White's Road to No. 118. By this time I had managed to save a little money, so I said to the boss that I would like to install at my cost, a telephone. No problem said he, but I will just as a courtesy, mention it to the PCC. I gather that it caused quite a stir. What does he need a telephone for? Our curates have never had one before and have always managed. I think it was only the timely intervention of Father Rowe that clarified for them that they were not being asked to pay, but only to give permission. When I was told of the background, I was furious and without further ado, I went down to the local branch office of the ASTMS trade union and joined on the spot. I hold a union card to this day, but more about that later on.

There was another and more amusing incident, just after I had moved into No. 118. I asked Father Rowe if he would mind me inviting the members of the local branch of the Mothers Union to come for a coffee morning. He looked at me as if to say, be it on your head, but then grinned and said, well go ahead then. The great day came and the ladies arrived with the 'Queen Bee' at the front escorted by her 'acolytes'. They were all wearing big and very heavy coats and placed them on my newly installed coat rack with the result that it came away from the wall and deposited all the coats in a big heap on the floor. "Do not worry," said the 'Queen Bee', "I will tell my husband to come and sort it out for you." He turned up the next morning, trying to make out that it gave him the greatest possible pleasure – and failing miserably! But in fairness, he did a real pukka job with a rough drawing, then a scale drawing followed by a provisional fitting and then a final fitting. Typical of the area, such matters were taken very seriously – 99% was not good enough; it had to be 100% every time and without fail. You cannot really criticise that.

The New Year's Eve party, I was told, was the highlight of the church Social calendar and was held in the church hall down the road. It started at 8.00pm and finished after midnight which we all toasted with a glass of dry sherry. There was no other alcoholic refreshment, but in fairness there was plenty of food, which saved me having to get myself a meal. The boss told me not to wear the dreaded clerical collar that night. It was quite refreshing to wear a tie again and feel that I was actually an ordinary human being.

It was then that I started to realise that there were one or two very attractive young ladies in the youth club and my mind started to work in other directions. Fortunately for me there was not going to be a last waltz that night, but there were floral button holes to be pinned into position and as most people know, I am pathetic at that sort of thing so I had to ask someone to help and the task fell on Hilary Birch who at that time was the Brownie Guider. She had been coming to church all her life together with her younger sister Heather and her mother. Hilary gave me a lovely smile, which I now know so very well!

But perhaps, now is the time to say a little about "The Boss". Father Anthony Rowe was a Coventry lad who just missed the war but was called up for National Service. When he came out, it was time for him to find a college in which to train for the full time ministry, but the catholic colleges were full up, so he went to St. John's Durham and never regretted it. He served his title curacy with the irrepressible and ever loquacious Father Henry at St. Luke's in Holbrooks, Coventry. I met Father Henry quite a few times; in fact I conducted a Good Friday Three Hours devotion for him, but boy, could he talk. In fairness, there always has been a little bit of

Holbrooks in me, especially as the custom there was always to preach a short sermon at the eight o'clock Eucharist, thus ensuring that the silent worshippers of that tradition had something to go home with.

Father Tony was a big man, about six feet, three inches tall and was extremely well-built. On one occasion, Bishop Cuthbert came to celebrate a mid week service and so we had three clerics there; Bishop, Priest and Deacon. Cuthbert was six feet seven inches tall and with a mitre on, he looked an absolute giant. I was six feet and looked a midget! I owe the boss a lot, it was a great sadness when he died but most of his former curates were able to be present at his funeral.

While on the subject of clerical personages, it might be worth describing a couple of Archdeacons. First of all there was the terrifying and powerful figure of Eric Buchan, Archdeacon of Coventry, known normally as Father B! Not a person to cross swords with and quite insensitive to the domestic requirements of a modern clerical family. He had served, as a chaplain, in the R.A.F. in the war and when he was vicar of St. Marks in Coventry he used to sleep on a camp bed in the vestry. I understand that on more than one occasion he was totally oblivious to the sight of the sky through a hole in the ceiling. Let alone any rain! Pat Morgan told me that when he called to see her and Alan, he made some very uncomplimentary remarks about the Welsh language and she had a go at him. He also used to preside at U.S.P.G. meetings and any clergy who could remotely be termed "catholic" were issued with a three-line whip to attend. I remember slinking in late to one meeting at Holy Trinity, Coventry and deftly taking a seat at the back. No such luck, because I had been seen, "My Wayward Son. Do come and sit in the front". He was just like a purring tiger before a tasty meal!

Ted Taylor was Archdeacon of Warwick and an old soldier. He used to write articles under the nom de plume of "Canon Fodder". For Ted, a spade was a spade and you knew where you stood, especially if he was delivering a wigging. When I had a few problems in the Stratford upon Avon Team, he was more than helpful and I could always go and see him for advice. He is remembered especially for his visitations, which were held in towns where there was a decent pub and he always bought a pint afterwards for the curates. I went to see him about a month before he died and he just said to me, "I kid you not mate, I do wonder about the clergy and I worry about them." Four weeks later he was dead. His service of thanksgiving in the cathedral on a Monday was packed with clergy.

Normally if anyone who took Monday as a day off and had been summoned to such an event, then they would have ignored the summons, but this was different and we all turned out.

To conclude this archdiaconal element, I call to mind a story that Tony Rowe told me of when he was a curate and had to attend the visitation in Holy Trinity, Coventry with Father Henry. In those days, a register was called, just like at school and you had to stand up and answer that you were present. Once that painful exercise had been completed, Father Henry said to his curate, "I am not staying to listen to this rubbish, come on follow me." He promptly crawled out on all fours followed by his faithful curate; both were wearing academic dress as prescribed by canon law. Happy days!

But to return to matters of a more delicate kind. I did some thinking and realised that I was now 30 years old. Was it right for me to get married? Was it the right thing to do? Was it vocational? I had pondered about a vocation to the religious life, but felt there was a danger that I might be running away from reality. Yet, when I had been accepted for training, the then Archbishop of Canterbury had asked me to at least consider if God was calling me to the celibate ministry, whether in parish life or in community. After due consideration, I felt that I was being called to the married state, so what to do? I had thought about one lady, but she rather blotted her copybook by going off with a married man in the parish. It clearly must be Hilary. So I consulted the boss. "What makes you think that she will want to go out with you?" he asked quizzically. I replied that body language etc had left me in no doubt. So I asked, and she said, yes. We went to the Dun Cow in Dunchurch, the following week we had lunch at the Plough in Ford on the edge of the Cotswolds and within a very short time we were unofficially engaged. We did not announce our engagement until the day of my First Mass, so both sets of parents had to keep it under wraps. I also had to formally ask permission from the bishop, but that did not cause a problem

The First Mass and preparations for marriage need to wait a bit, because I would like to say something about the new Bishop of Coventry. He could not have been more different than Cuthbert. John Gibbs was an educationalist and was a self taught man. His was the last episcopal appointment under the old system and it was rumoured that Harold Wilson had read a paper on current educational trends which impressed him, so to Coventry was John Gibbs sent. I liked John very much, he had been a Congregational Minister in the past and when a youngster, had started work with his parents, by selling fruit and veg from a barrow in the local market. He was masterful in assessing a situation and then delivering a thoughtful opinion with suggestions for future action.

Parish life has to carry on, even if the curate has been involved in surreptitious courting. The parish was very strong on pastoral work and this was based very much on a sacramental approach because the Blessed Sacrament was taken out to the sick on a very regular basis. Every Monday and Tuesday morning without fail, plus other days on a monthly basis, we went out on the rounds. We had weekly, fortnightly and monthly communicants and it was a wonderful ministry. At Christmas and Easter, we laid on a very special service for them at church and made strenuous efforts to arrange transport. Coffee was served afterwards and it gave an opportunity for the disabled and the sick to see their church again and catch up with local church news.

The youth club was my main concern. There were two groups, Saturday morning and Sunday night. The tradition was that those who wanted to come on Sunday night would make the effort to worship at evensong, and, for the most part, they did. I spent quite a lot of my time on youth matters. It was fairly traditional with snooker, table tennis, darts etc and had been in the past a bit of a marriage bureau. We had a great time together with walks in the summer to Canley Ford with its milk bar and cricket matches and even a rugby match. Visits to the fire station, the sewerage works and a night with the celestial stars and planets were always well attended. By now it was getting close to my priesting so the boss, mindful of his duties, suggested that we might go through the service a few times. This was very helpful, for although I had been liturgically trained by a top guy, it was always worth relating the academics to the reality of the parish. I was to be ordained on June 27th in the cathedral and this time the retreat was to be held at Offchurch, but I did take my own retreat with the Holy Name Sisters at Malvern Link. So the Feast of St. Peter arrived and I celebrated Holy Mass for the first time, but afterwards I announced my engagement and that shook the parish!

Chapter 7

FIRST MASS, MARRIAGE AND CONCLUSION OF CURACY AT HEARSALL COMMON

I celebrated a High Mass with my colleagues Geoff and Henry filling the Deacon and Sub Deacon spots. It was not just a question of getting the words and the actions correct, there was also the business of using incense, but the well trained servers were not going to let me get that wrong. Then afterwards there was the nice problem of facing the parishioners and explaining how I managed to do my courting without anyone knowing about it. What we had done, was to let our parents into the secret and then arrange for Hilary to be dropped up at Gibbet Hill, south Coventry where I would meet her and take her out for the day. With a bit of luck, we could slip back into the parish when it was dark, and nobody would know a thing. Needless to say, on either the first or second return, we bumped into Hilary's younger sister, Heather, but she kept her mouth closed. A Roman Catholic priest friend of mine was pleased to record that at least I was celibate when I celebrated mass for the first time; it was almost as if he was saying that I was orthodox! Incidentally, when a priest celebrates for the first time, there are one or two traditions to observe. The priest communicates his parents first and gives his mother a bouquet of flowers. I could not run to red roses, which was the usual thing to do, but I did make sure that there were plenty of red flowers and my father was more than happy to communicate at a very "Catholic Mass". There were speeches in the church hall and the exchange of gifts, it was all most gratifying and yet very humbling. However I was not finished as there must be three masses first time; of the Holy Spirit, For Our Lady and a Requiem, so I had more liturgical work to do, which took place during the mid week masses of the following week. So, I could now help out the boss with the Sunday services; there were three eucharists on a Sunday morning and then there was Evensong. The boss and I got into the habit of ensuring that whoever was celebrating, did not preach, so, although full vestments were the order of the day, the preacher wore surplice or cotta and stole.

I had said to Father Anthony some time ago that I was ready to preach each week. I remember him looking at me and saying, "Are you sure?" "No problem," I said. Mind you it was not long before he passed comment on my preaching as follows. At college I had been made aware of the riches of the old testament by an inspirational lecturer called Tony Barnard. I was so taken with these newly revealed scriptural riches that I always preached on the old testament until one day, the boss, said to me that I was to forgo the old testament for six months and preach on either the epistles, or preferably, the Gospels.

I still love to hear the old testament and especially the books of Exodus, Ruth and the minor prophets. They resonate with me in a very special way and inevitably I feel moved to comment on them. My favourite gospel is that of John; the prologue is magnificent and of course, not being one of the synoptic gospels, it has a different message. I find it a very priestly scripture.

Very soon the wedding day approached and we needed to make plans. Hilary would need some period of adjustment although she would continue her career as a local government officer. This was apparent when just after our engagement was announced there was a traditional parish event when we all sat on the top table and Hilary was told that she was expected to join this august gathering. She protested vigorously, but to no avail and had to leave her friends who had taken up station at the bottom end and move up higher (as it says in the gospels!). We were agreed on a Nuptial Mass. Heather would attend Hilary and Geoff was to be my best man. The date was set and we started the task of establishing a guest list. The honeymoon was very easily established. Hilary wanted to go to Switzerland; I wanted to return, so we soon agreed on the grand tour by train. Dead easy! Then there were the first few nights together before the flight to Basle, so we plumped for Chipping Norton where I had gone to school all those years ago. And then the big day came and I remember just walking across the road with my best man to be married, having of course, been over previously to say the morning office. Priestly duties did not go away.

The weather was not brilliant, in fact it rained as we were just about to get into the cars, but at least it was bright when we emerged from the Church to be greeted by a Brownie guard of honour and a press photographer. At the reception in Meriden, Grace was said by my old friend Bishop John Daly who had come with his faithful sister, Barbara. Hilary had been fairly traditional in her choice of dress, whereas I had decided to hire traditional clerical wear, which meant a special trip down to London to visit Moss Bros. When I put the gear on, I looked like an Edwardian Undertaker and Geoff ultimately compounded the whole sartorial experience by wearing the gear to a fancy dress party later that night in his parish. The following day we knelt at the altar together in Chipping Norton Parish Church! Very soon it was time to fly off to Switzerland, the land of mountains and lakes, rack and pinion railways and cow bells in the alpine meadows. All very idyllic. When we were in Lucerne, it was Ascension Day, so we found out the local parish of the Old Catholic Church where we were made very welcome and the priest spoke good English. In fact, outside the church there was a big sign saying that the Old Catholic Church was in full communion with the Church of England and the rest of the Anglican Communion. The way it was put amounted to saying that they had nothing whatsoever to do with the Bishop of Rome. All too soon we were heading back home and I was on duty the next morning to celebrate the Eucharist at 9.00am. By now I was beginning to start thinking of my next move. Second curacy or first incumbency. That was the question.

At the end of the day, I was learning so much about being a parish priest that it would pay me to stay on and make it a four year curacy. There was some manoeuvring from the diocese about a second curacy, but they backed off and left me to get on with things. In any case there was still a lot to do and Father Anthony had a few bouts of sickness, which meant that I took charge and again learned more and more, especially about leadership. I did ask the boss if he would mind me organising a Church Fête. Quite honestly what had been served up in previous years was nothing short of pathetic and so my parishioner and good friend Heather Partis joined me in my endeavours, and we decided to think big. First of all we needed a big field and to our delight, the Roman Catholics could not have been more helpful with their school being ideally situated for our requirements. We made a provisional booking of the Red Arrows, but this had to be called off because of the immediacy of the high voltage overhead wire of the railway track nearby. Never mind, I made sure of a small narrow gauge railway which could be set up and taken down again fairly quickly. Donkey rides were a novel addition to the normal fare also a coconut shy and of course there were the usual stalls plus a 'Greasy Garry' hot food stall.

It was a great day, good for relationships with the local community and good for the funds. Everyone was happy and all agreed that we must do it again. But this was not to be, because I had an offer of another post, which I actually turned down, but more was in the pipeline. It did not start too well because I was told that a new curate would be coming to Hearsall Common so really I ought to move on. Blackmail? I leave you to decide, but the boss came up trumps and made it quite clear that the house was mine and any other curate would have to go into digs. Then I had a phone call from Ted Taylor telling me that I was to be offered my first incumbency at Shottery. Great news indeed!

The situation at Shottery was that after many years of being a placement for a senior curate at Holy Trinity Stratford, the powers that be had decided that Shottery should have its own vicar within a Team Ministry. The drafting of the Order in Council was a bit watery to say the least. I was to be a vicar in the Team Ministry, but I was also to be Vicar of Shottery. There were to be full churchwardens, an independent PCC, the payment of diocesan quota to be the responsibility of Shottery, and not Stratford upon Avon and just to be different there was to be a Group Council. Other than that, it was to be nice and straightforward. The population was about 9,000 and there was an almost new vicarage opposite thatched cottages, it seemed to be heavenly. I did actually know something about Shottery, because I had once met at the fire station, the curate of the day, called Elevet Jones. He had been a Welsh Baptist minister, but seen the light and been ordained into the Church of England. He was very much on the high side and was remembered with much love and affection. His wife had been a professional ballroom dancer and he could shimmy round the floor himself. But of course, Shottery is well known for being the village where Anne Hathaway's cottage is situate, so I would be well into Shakespeare. It seemed like a dream come true, and basically it was.

But back to legalities, it was decided that I should meet the churchwardens with Hilary as soon as possible. We went over one evening and met Norman and Ted, plus their wives. We had a convivial evening together, but I remembered what my boss had told me, which was basically, play it like poker, don't show all your cards, keep them guessing. It was good advice. Various questions were asked such as my attitude to ecumenical affairs, did I visit and most important of all, would I have any objections to the practice of the vicar taking services from behind the bar of the Bell Inn at Harvest and Christmas? As most of you will have established by now, this latter question would clearly not present a problem. So it was agreed that we would think about it, discuss with friends of discretion, pray about it and make contact at the end of the week! Clearly my poker face had worried Norman. Both he and Ted wanted me to come, but Norman could not resist phoning me to ask if I had any problems that needed resolving. By then, Hilary and I had decided that we would love to go to Shottery, so I was able to impart the good news to Norman.

There were other people to see as well, including Canon Peter Barnes who was the Team Rector. We came from opposite ends of the theological candle and did not always agree, but I had a healthy respect for him and he was canny in the best sense of the word and did not try to mould colleagues into his own image. So we started to make plans. I needed to sign off from St Mary Magdalen's and agree a date for my last service and to agree a date for my licensing. We were also advised to move first and then take a holiday before licensing, and that turned out to be very good advice indeed. I remember preaching at my last service on the words, "and the waters covered the earth" so it was off to south warwickshire and a new life away from the city.

We had scarcely moved in before Norman turned up to enquire if we were doing anything that night. I said that we might just go out for a drink down the road, to which the reply was, "I'll pick you up in an hour's time." We went to the Shakespeare Hotel and it was all very different from Coventry. On another night we were introduced to the locals at the Bell Inn, followed by the Three Witches and then we flew out to Italy for a gorgeous holiday in Sorrento with much good wine and good company. Funnily enough, on that visit, we made friends with two elderly ladies from a branch of the Mothers' Union in Chester Diocese. A few years later they all came down to see us and it was good to renew the friendship formed in Sorrento. But all too soon we returned to start anew.

Chapter 8

SHOTTERY IN THE TEAM MINISTRY AND THE FREEHOLD OF SHOTTERY ST. ANDREW

One of the things that I had not really been prepared for was the conduct and chairing of PCCs, so it was not very long before this particular pleasure came my way for the first time. However once the summer holidays were behind us, we got down to business. The beauty about Shottery was, that being a young parish, it was open to all sorts of ideas and it was a great place to try things out. There were occasions when we jointly came a cropper, but there were plenty of times when we jointly enjoyed some great successes. I remember a very early PCC which was held on October 1st 1979. It was Ted's birthday and being Ted, who was very Welsh, he had said that he was holding a Welsh Jam Party down at the Bell Inn after the meeting. Needless to say that there is nothing more guaranteed to shorten a meeting than the promise of free food and drink, so we set to with a merry heart. But one or two things have stuck in my memory and I can still see Harry Berry waiting outside the vicarage until precisely 7.30pm when he then came into the meeting. At the end of the meeting I told the PCC that Hilary was expecting our first child, so there was double cause for celebration. Harry Berry went home from the Bell, a very happy man. He went into his bedroom where his wife had already gone to bed and said, "You'll never guess what, Hilary is going to have a baby," and promptly dropped dead! That was my first serious call out, so to speak and the funeral was one week later on October 8th, which was my birthday. It was a big turn out and it was my first big funeral on my own.

It so often happens, that following on from something like a sudden death, there is an awakening of faith. Harry's daughter Carole Taylor went on to become PCC secretary, churchwarden and PCC treasurer and is still very involved with the church after all these years. I made a point of putting bereavement visiting at the top of my priorities and it reaped countless dividends. There was the rather useful connection of also being chaplain at Stratford hospital, where I had a very fulfilling ministry. I did not like the idea at all when it was first put to me, but then it transpired that the payment from the hospital for services rendered went to make up my stipend, so there was not much that I could do about it. However I was not to worry because after just one visit, I was totally smitten with it and spent many happy hours over there.

Perhaps this is the time to tell a few stories about my time there. I remember reporting at the sister's office on the men's medical ward and coming into the presence of the fearsome Sister Gunn. "What can I do for you Padre?" She said rather powerfully. I said that I would like to give communion to one of her patients and tentatively suggested a time. "No problem," said she who was very mighty, "I will see you then." I made jolly sure that I was on time and it was an amazing experience, because, Sister Gunn just rose from her desk and swept onto the ward, she said nothing at all and those who were not required just melted away. A table appeared by the bedside, a clean linen cloth, a bowl of fresh flowers, I was bowed in and the curtains were closed behind me. Not much doubt in establishing who the boss there was. I understand that the consultants treated her with the utmost respect and deference. Another story which is worth telling related to the night that I had a phone call from one of the wards to ask if I could go up and administer last rites. This I did, and the patient was fully conscious and told me that I had, "done it very well". She then gave me a £5 note. Before I went, I popped into the office to see Sister who was of the very definite opinion that the patient would not last the night, so I went home to return fairly early next morning. When I came back on the ward the bed had been stripped, so I naturally thought that the worst had happened, but no, there had been a remarkable recovery. The patient had asked for a cooked breakfast and was ready to go home! It did me a lot of good and I took on board a new nickname, which was obviously, "miracle worker". When I eventually left Shottery, it took me a very long time to go round the wards and say goodbye. But it was not all work; there was some play as well. I am not sure how it happened, but I found myself becoming chairman of the staff social club, which had the added advantage of running a licensed bar with drinks at very low prices. I used to take my turn behind the bar and even Matron came in for the occasional sherry. But one night things got out of hand. The women's medical ward decided to dress up and have a party, so some of the old ladies went out for the night to the club, which was just across the passageway. The mother of the car mechanic who serviced my car was one of them and thoroughly enjoyed herself. Unfortunately, one of the Staff nurses got a bit tipsy and an edict came down from on high that there would be no further excursions.

But to return to the parish. We celebrated the birth of our first son, Mark Andrew on April 19th 1980 and he was subsequently baptised on June 29th, which was a very special anniversary for me. I brewed a beer for the occasion and invited the whole parish to join us. There was not much beer left when we finally finished. When Hilary had brought Mark home from the Monroe Devis Maternity Home on her birthday, it unfortunately clashed with my first AGM, but fortunately for me, the meeting did not go on too long as everyone knew of the homecoming. By now we were beginning to have some very pleasant problems, such as what to do with more people coming to church? Now I am the first to say, that it is so easy to become self important at a time such as this and to be guilty of pride, especially when people start saying complimentary things to you and comparing you with your predecessor. Beware, is what I would say to a young incumbent and never forget the basic principle that your ministry is to prepare for the ministry of whoever will come after you. If you do a lot of harvesting, then someone will have done a lot of sowing. Despite the spiritual dangers for me, we did need to do something and this meant re-arranging the Sunday morning. If I remember correctly, the service times were 8.00am and 10.30am, so we slipped in an additional service at 9.30am. We then had the problem that I will never ever have again of fielding complaints from those who were waiting outside for the 9.30am service to finish before they could get in for the 10.30am service. I remember saying that they wouldn't get that anywhere else.

The next project was to consider the possibility of a church hall, although there was no possibility of being able to afford a permanent building, would the local council go along with a portakabin, suitably clad? Yes was the answer, after some negotiating. Annoyingly we then were told that we had to go through the whole business again and apply for a faculty. I was not best pleased, but for one reason or another, I had recently asked for a scale map of the church building and surrounding land. After a cursory glance, I saw the answer to my prayers. Where the portakabin was to go was not on consecrated land. I had the greatest possible pleasure in telling the diocesan authorities that a faculty was not required, so we went ahead and ordered. The bits and pieces arrived on the feast of the Epiphany and there was a snow blizzard. Eventually, the bits and pieces were put together. But we needed a supply of water, so a few of us dug a trench and then got builders to put in a supply pipe, with connections. Finally, one Sunday afternoon, I went outside with my old clothes on and filled it in with the correct grade of shingle/stones. The first parish group to use it was the Ladies Fellowship and they voted it a great success. Later, we invited Bishop John to perform a formal opening and he duly obliged, for which duties he received a bottle of malt whisky!

Yes, we had a Ladies Fellowship, but we did not have a Mothers' Union Branch. Shottery must have been the only church in the diocese to have a branch of the Church of England Men's Society and not have a branch of the Mothers' Union. I became diocesan chaplain for my sins and went to many an annual conference and although I thoroughly enjoyed myself, it was fairly obvious that the writing was on the wall. The decision to call off the Annual Conference which that year would have been in Coventry was taken in my vicarage. All that was left was to perform the last rites. What a crying shame. I met some first rate christians, but as I was to contemplate at a later date; two world wars and the busyness of synodical government did not help. The very least I could do was to instigate the commencement of a new branch of the Mothers' Union and it absolutely took off. It is good to know that it is still in fine fettle, some 30 years later.

Needless to say I was active in other pastures. I had been going down to the Bell Inn at Shottery for some time when I noticed that Len Payne the landlord had brought in some real ale. One thing led to another and before I realised it, I had called an inaugural meeting to see if a branch of CAMRA might be formed. It certainly could and we had a good time together. I was not able to go off on the various trips that they arranged, but it was wonderful to be invited back for the 30th anniversary celebrations.

We were still having nice problems to solve and now the whole business of car parking began to rear its head. If we could buy a strip of land next door from the squire, we would be able to access a brand new car park and not have to drive up the vicarage drive. It would also give us a lot more space and the possibility of further growth could become a probability, although that would be for someone else to sort out. So I went to see the squire and walked up to the big house from the church along his private path through the woods. He certainly wanted his pound of flesh plus all costs, but somehow or other, we managed to find the money and the deal went ahead. Our own solicitors would not charge, but received a crate of wine, and the vendor's solicitors, (senior partner was a member of CMS) actually paid us what he had received from the vendor. Happy days indeed.

Ecumenical matters were very much centred on Stratford, but it was clear to me that ecumenical endeavour with the Methodist church up on Bishopton estate would be very productive, so I went round to make friends with the minister. He was all for it and I also found out that he was a professional musician in his own right. So we decided to hold an act of worship in the assembly Hall of Bishopton primary school and we circulated the entire estate with our intentions. It went an absolute bomb and we were packed out. At the beginning of the service, Peter Smith and I sat at opposite ends of a bench. By the end of the service we had both moved a little more towards the centre. We decided to go for a Local Ecumenical Project; the only problem was the C of E which told us that we must wait while they set up a structure to control us. I wonder what Wesley would have said? Those were halcyon days indeed. We had a couple of baptisms and a confirmation which respected the two different traditions. Then came the big decision. We could have a fulltime minister and as the Church Army students were on a mission with us at that time, we started to look in that direction. We had a lot of work to do, but the two church bodies worked well together and sorted out the cash. I persuaded the council to let us rent a house up on the estate and then we appointed Steve Payne as our first minister and a sizeable number of Shottery parishioners went down to Southwark Cathedral for his licensing as a Church Army Captain. We had a great time and had lunch at a typical London pub with its own micro brewery. It was absolutely tipping down with rain, but we sheltered outside under a big railway girder and enjoyed good beer, good food and above all, good fellowship. What more could you ask for? Steve soon made a name for himself and he was a first rate colleague. He is now ordained and serving in Exeter Diocese.

Service attendance was well on the way upwards. I must admit that today I would not want to provide so many services, but it certainly ensured the punters coming through the front door. I remember that on one particular Sunday, I actually led nine services. There were always people wanting to say Morning Prayer with me at 7.30am, and then followed communion services at 8.00am, 9.30am and 10.30am. There then followed a baptismal service at 12.30pm and after lunch, it was across to the estate for the ecumenical service. Evensong was at 6.00pm followed by communion and then it was down to the hospital to sing the praises of the Lord around the wards. I have to say, that I was shattered. There were of course other services and I introduced Shottery to the liturgical delights of Holy Week and especially the paschal celebrations on the Saturday night. But Palm Sunday presented the perfect opportunity to witness to the local community, because one of my parishioners had a donkey and was willing to bring it to church. In fairness to Zillah (the farmer's wife), she had to drag this creature up Bordon Hill and down to the car park at the Bell Inn where a procession started. The choir turned out in all their finery, the wardens carried their staves and just about everyone tagged on with the result that the church was packed. The donkey was reasonably well behaved and I do not remember it ever leaving a sample in the road!

The prayer life of the parish took a definite step forward when we decide to set up a prayer matrix for the parish, for the diocese, for the country and for the world. We designed a special prayer card and I sent a copy to every anglican convent or monastery in the UK, asking for prayer, especially at a time which we agreed would act as a focus. I received some wonderful letters from abbots, abbesses, priors etc and it was quite obvious that a lot of people were praying for the parish. At the same time I had encouraged parishioners to send prayer cards to their friends throughout the country and throughout the world. So we put up a couple of big maps at the back of the church and stuck on the replies that we had received with a straight line being drawn to the actual place on the map. I must confess that it looked quite dramatic. The maps remained in church until after I had moved on to the next parish.

I used to go into church every morning and evening to say the daily offices, I also took the opportunity to ring the bell and tell the village what I was doing. Initially there were a few ribald comments, but fairly soon they all got used to it and, if for any reason I was away and the bell did not ring, then I soon knew about it. I also introduced the parish to the saints and the celebration of the Holy Eucharist on their special days. I may not have done a roaring trade, but the practice was kept up and St. Andrews Day presented another opportunity to go one step on, because we could invite a guest preacher and lay on refreshments afterwards. It seemed appropriately diplomatic to invite Archdeacon Ted Taylor for my first Patronal Festival especially as I needed his support to create a garden of remembrance up on the top field. There was not much problem, because he gave me some first rate advice in how to approach a faculty application and then spoke very strongly for us at the inevitable diocesan advisory committee. I remember what he said in his sermon about Andrew being the first missionary because he brought his brother to meet Jesus!

During this time I was pleased to support a couple of enquiries from young men about the possibility of ordination and they were subsequently ordained, which was most gratifying. On another occasion, a young ordinand moved in next door and asked if he could practice the organ from time to time. He was an associate of the Royal College of Organists and certainly knew how to play; he also used to join me for the morning offices. Nigel is now Vicar of Crediton in Devon. We keep in touch and it was good to see him and Tina with their young family a couple of years ago.

Chapter 9

MID TERM AT SHOTTERY

There are still a few characters who I would like to mention, but before I do so, one further story about Father B. I had been involved with both USPG and CMS for a few years and had actually gone to Partnership House in London to discuss the possibilities of a placement abroad in the missionary field. It appeared that I was being lined up for a parish in Zambia and the formal letter was sent out. Unfortunately, the USPG had the wrong address and I never received the letter, I therefore never made contact with that department and they did not make contact with me, so obviously it was not to be. However on one occasion, I attended a meeting of council and had decided to take the usual liquid lunch, and as I was walking down Tufton Street, I heard a loud and familiar voice. "My wayward son!" I could not get out of it, there was nowhere to hide or escape to; one moment I was going in one direction and the next moment I was going backwards as I was gathered up and carried off to the restaurant of the Church Commissioners where I had a first rate lunch with the compliments of Father B. Perhaps it was worth it.

Back to more local ecclesiastical personages: George Burgess retired from Alveston and moved into Shottery. He loved his golf and was invariably on the course with my colleague the Team Rector, Canon Peter Barnes. He was good fun and fairly laid back. He had a first rate and memorable ministry in Longford, Coventry before moving to Alveston, where he is remembered with much love and affection. Then there was Lionel Daffern. Lionel retired to a small bungalow and started to worship with us. Very gentle, very deferential, he was a Mothers' Union delight. His hobbies were baking, sewing, knitting and embroidery! He had been Vicar of St. Thomas in Coventry, a church which had eventually been knocked down. It was next door to Chapelfields, so I knew the area. Then one day I found out that there was another side to Lionel as a letter which was addressed to him came to the vicarage instead and after his name were the letters, D.F.C. I made further enquiries and it transpired that he had been commissioned in the Royal Air Force and had flown low level craft, attacking shipping at about 50 feet with torpedoes. As he said to me, most of his friends were shot down, either by German/Italian shipping or if they managed to deliver their attack and get up into the skies, then there were fighter planes waiting for them. It appears that he got his decoration for protecting a colleague who had aborted his attack because he had been badly shot up. Lionel radioed him up to have another go and that he, Lionel would fly parallel and take the flak. Needless to say, the attack was successfully delivered and Lionel survived to be ordained a priest.

Then there was Bishop Vernon who had been Bishop of Sodor and Man and he must have known that a few of us, including me tended to rewrite his Episcopal title. Vernon Nicholls was a bouncy character and there were times when you needed to stand up to him, but he was a first rate colleague and very much a man's man. He had married a local girl from Shipston on Stour and made his name as Vicar of Walsall and Archdeacon of Birmingham. He was also big in the Masons which did not go down well with everyone, but I believe in taking people as I find them and he was good value. I had actually met him at the hospital when his wife was in for an operation. As chaplain, I received a summons that communion was required, so I toddled off to the ward and rather unctuously, kissed the episcopal ring, which he absolutely loved, and then I suggested that he really ought to pronounce the absolution. "No," was the sonorific reply. "But," I protested, "I am only a priest." "I don't care. You are doing it." There was no point in arguing. Bishop Vernon decided that when I was on holiday, he would do some parish visiting on my behalf. I cannot remember being asked, but that is irrelevant as he decided to call on the newly arrived Lionel. As you have probably gathered, that irrespective of war service, Lionel just wanted the quiet life. The last thing he wanted was a visit from a bouncy Bishop telling him that there were all sorts of things going on in this very lively parish and that he could have a most fulfilling retirement ministry. I am told that Lionel sighed a very big sigh.

By this time, Hilary was beginning to discover new channels for her to pursue, starting with her big love of Guiding. It didn't take long before she was involved with Brownies again and there was also the toddlers club around at the village hall. As Mark was growing up rapidly it was decided that we would like to add to the family, so Peter James was born on July 2nd, 1982 and Mark had a little brother to play with. The two were very different and are so to this day. They occasionally fought and there were the odd scraps to deal with and in fairness it was Hilary who took the lead in these domestic matters. I was invariably never around being out at meetings. I bitterly regret not being there when I was needed because I basically missed their growing up, totally and utterly. I would strongly advise all young clergy who are married to be very careful in this respect. Peter was baptised at Harvest time and there is a photograph of me with Peter, Mark and Dad: it is very meaningful to me as within one week my father had died and for once I had to try and deal with grief at a personal level. We had gone down to Kent to see Heather and Geoff, but there was a phone call that night telling me that I needed to return very quickly to Leamington Spa. My brother-in-law very kindly drove me all the way back at the dead of night through the centre of London and it was decided that Hilary would return the next day with the boys.

When we got to my mother's house I was told the sad news, but of course it did not really strike home. I took mother back to the vicarage and when Hilary returned with the boys, I remember Mark giving his Grandma a big kiss. I then decided to go to evensong which was being taken by another retired priest, Canon Raymond Cyster, who told everyone what had happened and conducted the service in his normal dignified and very sensitive manner. It was during the singing of the hymn, "The Day thou gavest Lord is Ended" that I broke down and started to cry in my own church. It was a very moving experience. The funeral arrangements now needed my attention which gave me something positive to do. It was clearly going to be a fire brigade funeral with full honours. In the old days the coffin would have been put on the back of an old appliance and draped with the union flag. There were not any of those appliances left, so it was decided to have a last turn out with all the current fleet out on the driveway at HQ in immaculate condition and with the sirens and lights going full blast as we passed by. Then we needed to remind ourselves that dad was a practicing Roman Catholic, even though he had received his last communion from my hands at the baptism of Peter. The Roman Catholic church at St. Peter's Leamington Spa could not have been more helpful. I arrived on the evening before the funeral with my mother for a reception into church and a requiem mass. I decided to wear my soutane, so I must have looked very, very catholic! Soon there was a revving and a squeal of brakes and a mini clubman did a handbrake skid and parked itself in a slot which was reserved for the clergy. Three scruffs got out. One of the scruffs came over to me and (in very cultivated tones) said, "Good evening Father, I understand that you are celebrating the mass for Mr. Capron?" "I think you've got that wrong." I said. "I am an Anglican priest and there is no way that I would be allowed to do so." "I know," said the scruff, "I am the Parish Priest." There followed a lively discussion in which I was once again offered the opportunity to celebrate mass, but as I said to the Parish Priest, it would soon get back and he would be in serious trouble. We compromised with me taking a fair amount of the Liturgy of the Word and then sprinkling and censing the coffin at the end. The funeral next day was attended by many colleagues as well as family and friends and all went well and we all went out for lunch on the Sunday. On the Monday I was back on duty and had to take two funerals which both ended up at the crematorium. As I led the mourners out of the chapel to the area where people congregate with their families, there, lying on the ground, were the flowers that had been on my father's coffin.

By now, Mark had celebrated his fourth birthday and was looking forward to starting at the local school. Shottery C of E primary school was a delightful institution right in the heart of the old village. I used to go in and take morning assembly there and I was also chairman of the governors. The previous headmistress was quite a lady – Sarah – and boy could she doll herself up. We got on very well, but she had taken over from a very formidable lady called, Mona Fortescue, who was very much one of the traditional village heads. Nobody was going to argue with her, but she worshipped with me in her retirement and was absolutely charming. She was one of five retired headteachers who came to the 8.00am service. Needless to say, I was on my very best behaviour. I well remember the very first day that Mark started at School. The weather had been atrocious the night before and when we took Mark down to school proudly wearing his new uniform, we also took Peter for the first hour.

We had now been in Shottery a few years and one day I decided to count up the communicants and see if they were going up. I had a slight shock when I found out that they were plateauing. Perhaps I should start looking for pastures new? It was a long shot, but as I had always had an inkling that I might like to go up to the northeast, I decided to go and look at a team ministry near Stockton on Tees at Thornaby. It was a no go for me. The previous team rector had decided to go back into Insurance broking, yet retaining a permission to officiate, and buying a flashy sports car which was regularly seen in the parish. Another priest could not cope with the realities of life and another was a bit of a Dell Boy character. No Way! I wrote formally and said, "thank you, but no thank you." A few weeks later, I received a letter from my old friend Stephen Pedley who said that he had heard I had been in the area and that I had done the right thing to keep well clear.

When I got home I went to have a chat with Keith Arnold the Bishop of Warwick. We began to explore the actual structure of the team ministry. By that time there had been a new team rector put in place, needless to say, nobody had consulted with me and I was only the team vicar. I was also finding it very difficult to relate effectively with Stratford. Bishop Keith started to go down the line of suggesting that Shottery should now become a separate benefice in its own right with the vicar holding freehold. This would mean breaking up the Team Ministry, but I could see that a few people down the road would not be too happy with that one. I was still being referred to as "The Curate" even though there had been a Vicar of Shottery for close on seven years. Bishop Keith said that he would write to the Team Rector of Holy Trinity and see what he had to say about his suggestion. He might even like to discuss it with his wardens and PCC. This he failed to do, in fact the letter from the bishop was filed away and nobody else saw it. After some time, I went back to Bishop Keith as I had heard nothing, however he had picked up what had actually happened and tipped off the wardens, who I knew quite well. It was decided that I should drive across the river bridge one night and go to see them. We had a good meeting and they were both very positive about the suggestion. The next thing for them to do was to ask their rector what the devil was going on. I was not invited to that meeting, which was just as well, because I gathered there were fireworks, but to cut a long story short, the processes were soon put in place to apply for an Order in Council.

There were no objections at the Shottery end and I think that the team rector was probably told not to interfere. Eventually an official looking envelope arrived in which the legal documents made it clear that Her Majesty in Council was graciously pleased etc and that the operative date would be April 1st 1979. On the due date, I rang the church bell vigorously at Morning Prayer and in the evening we celebrated a Sung Eucharist together and I preached on the theme of being, "Fools for Christ". However, I had still been thinking about the northeast and my feelings had been reinforced when I attended a "Catholic Renewal Conference" at Loughborough University. There were a lot of Australians present and they were great fun in the bar after Benediction. But there was one particular priest sitting there by himself who was wearing a Fosters lager sweatshirt. We called him Father Foster and it transpired that he was Vicar of Newton Aycliffe up in County Durham and he told me all about it. Some months later, the said parish came up in the clearing system so I decided to apply. I was met by the wardens off the train at Darlington and whisked off to meet the archdeacon. Derek Hodgson was a sacramental evangelical and a local lad from Shildon. He was held in great regard by the wardens and I was told that there was no way they would upset him. What he said went. Not out of fear, but out of respect. I remember him telling me that if I decided to come, (and they were happy for me to do so), I would need to establish a bolt hole and get away from the town. It had seen off quite a few of its priests either through death or serious illness. It was then decided that I should go home and come back with Hilary. I am always very grateful to Hilary for being prepared to come with me. To leave the thatched cottages of Shottery, the village, our friends and our family and go up north to the Kingdom of Northumbria. Not many vicar's wives would have done that!

Well. We did come back and this time I was taken off to see the bishop himself. David Jenkins was not exactly the most popular bishop in the establishment, but I warmed to him. A superb brain, yes, but also he was very strong on pastoral matters. After a few cursory questions he clearly had made up his mind and the parish was formerly offered to me, with the proviso that as so few people had looked at it, the presentation of the benefice was now time expired so the Archbishop of York would write to me in due course. So, other than a few legalities it was all done and dusted and we went back to have a celebratory drink with my new colleagues. But I now needed to go back, tell my bishop and most difficult of all, tell the parish.

After a few weeks, and having replied in the affirmative to the Archbishop of York, it was agreed that the announcement could be made. So, with a heavy heart, I imparted the news to Shottery and there was

Capron's Garage and Fire Brigade, Minehead.

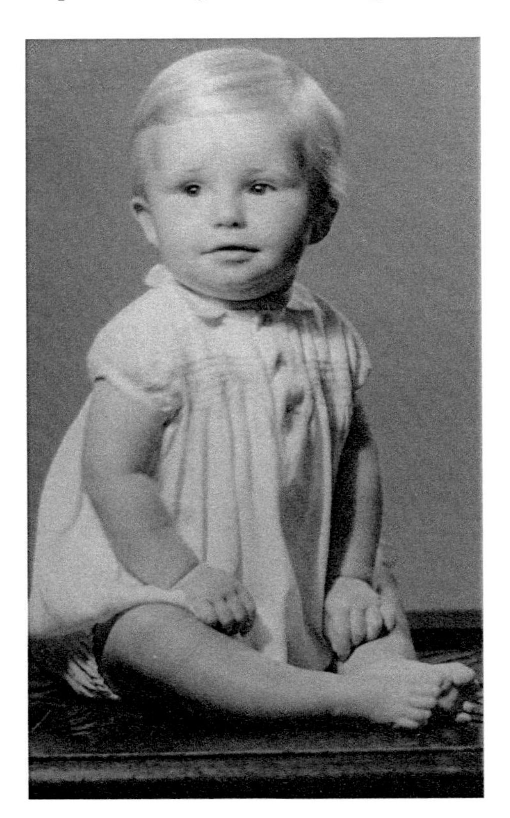

Early years.

At Minehead in the early '50s.

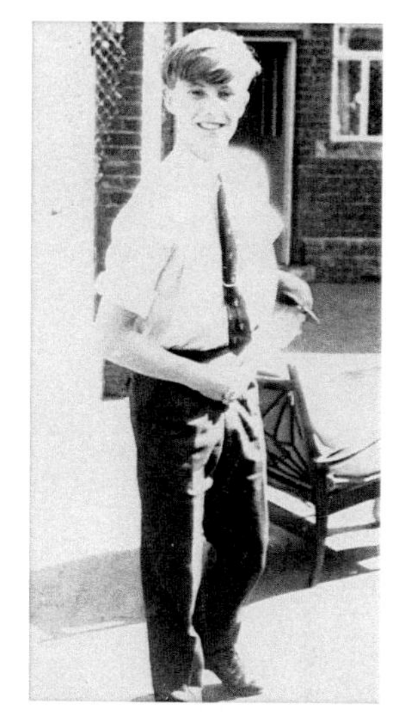

At Rugby School.

21st Birthday Party.

'The day I told them'.

Dad receives OBE at Buckingham Palace, 1973.

Ordination to the Diaconate.

Amateur Dramatics during Curacy.

First Mass.

Wedding Day, 1977.

Open University Graduation, 1980.

Three generations of Caprons, 1982.

Institutions and Inductions

Shottery, 1979.

Newton Aycliffe, 1986.

Alcester, 1995 (after completion of new Rectory).

The family at Newton Aycliffe.

'Best pint in town!'

Silver anniversary as a Priest,
with mother 2001.

60th Birthday at Woodstock.

Honorary Canon of Coventry Cathedral, 2007.

stunned silence. People could not understand why I was going all the way up north when I had just been inducted to the freehold of Shottery St. Andrew. Incidentally, I had found out that the folk in Newton Aycliffe had thought the same thing. Why does he want to leave thatched cottages etc and come up here? Anyway, we now had to do a lot of things fairly quickly as the Durham end were thinking about an institution before the end of November. This meant going back up to County Durham a few times and measuring up as well as sorting school out for the boys. I also needed to help in the process of appointing my successor, by sitting down and writing out a "customary", so that he could at least have some idea of what went on and how I went about it. Any changes that he felt were necessary, could then be made with the understanding that he knew all about the past. It was also time to go round and say personal goodbyes to a lot of people, and during this time, the PCC had discussions with the bishop and others about a successor. By the time I actually drove out of the parish, it had more or less been signed and sealed. But now for just one deviation before the finale.

For some years I felt there was need for a course rugby club in Stratford upon Avon and so I formed Shottery RFC. It is quite simple really, you find a pub, you find a field and a changing room and you persuade a brewery to buy a set of shirts. The first game was graced with the presence of the Chair of the District Council and she thoroughly enjoyed the wine that was laid on for her consumption afterwards. It turned out to be money well spent, because when the magistrates decided to be mean minded and not grant us an extension at the Bell Inn, I was able to use her influence at the second attempt and it sailed through court. I remember the first try, the first disciplinary inquest, the first party and more seriously the first charity raising function when we donated a television set to the hospital. The badge is the cross of Saint Andrew with a gold rugby ball and a gold bell, for obvious reasons. They are still in action after 26 years, but more of them in another chapter.

When I had first started at Shottery all those years ago, I remember during my first service, leaning over to Bob Wright the tenor who was next to me and saying that we really must sing something together sometime. During the first hymn of the service when I had announced my impending departure, I whispered to Bob, that if we did not do something in the next few weeks, we would never do it. So we sat down to sort out what we might sing. It was felt that at the final party would be appropriate, but what to sing? In the end, we decided to sing that famous duet from the Pearl Fishers by Bizet called, "Au fond du Temple Saint" set in Ceylon as it was then. I must confess that I have never heard anything else from that particular opera, but never mind, it is still a classic piece. Fortunately we were able to persuade the organist at the URC Church to be our accompanist and also to keep us on the straight and narrow. We met at Bob Wright's house and being a west country man like me, he was fond of the fermented juice of the apple, which was frequently dispensed. We had many happy hours practicing and it looked as if it would be all right on the night.

Meanwhile we had to get estimates for the move and I needed to go up with a friend and lay some carpets which meant hiring in a van. That took three days, but was well worth doing. The day for the actual move had to be fixed and arrangements for the boys to stay on at school until just before the removal van was due to leave. Then it was arranging the party which was fixed for the evening of Remembrance Sunday 1986 at the village hall, but before this bittersweet evening, we had a delightful evening out and it is worth telling the story. One of my regulars was the cocktail bar manager at the Welcombe Hotel and he invited me and Hilary to be his personal guests for an evening. He had even brought in a barrel of real ale just for me! When the evening came to a close he asked if I would like a special drink to finish off and I said that I would like an Armagnac. "Which year were you born in?" he asked, so I told him and the waiter behind the bar was told to deliver up a generous measure of a 1945 Armagnac. There isn't any left. Well then, open a 1944 bottle. It has not been opened. "Open it" was the order, and it was absolutely exquisite.

The day of the party came and the duet went very well under the circumstances. All that remained was for the final service, last sermon and goodbye on the Church steps. There were tears all round and it is not something that I could cope with on a frequent basis. We drove out the next day and as the removal van drove away, it took the gate post with it!

Chapter 10

THE KINGDOM OF NORTHUMBRIA

Newton Aycliffe is a new town of about 30,000 persons, just north of Darlington, in County Durham. It was part of the Aycliffe and Peterlee Development Corporation set up by Harold Wilson when he was President of the Board of Trade in the 1945 Attlee Government. The town and adjoining industrial estate was built on an ammunition dump, close to a very famous railway, which made it all the more fascinating to me. I speak of course of the Stockton and Darlington Railway which in September 1825 put on the rails, the first steam hauled, public, passenger train in the world. That in itself would be enough to make any town famous, but there was more to come, because the very first junction between two independent railways also was set in the town and the Clarence railway was the scene of one of the very first electrification schemes between the two wars. It was also one of the first to finish, and all overhead gantries were taken down as part of the war effort. After the war, the railway authorities went one step further and took up the whole line, but at least the vestiges of the old S & D still remain. We should also be grateful to the local Quaker and Roman Catholic communities who got fed up with the prevarications of the local established, Anglican, property owning classes and combined together to ensure that they were out manoeuvred and so the railway was built.

When the town was first built, the authorities set very high standards in respect of those who might want to live there. Prospective couples were visited in their current homes and the garden was inspected for tidiness. Upon actually picking up the keys and moving in, the lucky couple would be visited on a regular basis for interview and inspection. If standards were not maintained, then the threat of eviction was usually brought to bear. Being a Labour controlled authority, it was not deemed expedient for there to be any hint of private enterprise, so even the Chief Executive had his own rent book. But, as is so often the case in such circumstances, there were going to be differences and so there were council houses and there were COUNCIL HOUSES. The wardens told me somewhat wickedly that when the conservative government forced all councils to allow their tenants to buy their own houses, all the local politicians voted against it, but, when it became law, they were first in the queue to buy their own. Has anything changed, I ask myself?

You could always tell when you got near to Newton Aycliffe, because when you passed through the village of Aycliffe you could smell it. The chemical works poured out some quite obnoxious smells and then you turned left off the A167 onto the estate to find a widespread town where a lot of effort had been made to brighten the place up. Certainly quite a lot of concrete had been used, especially in the town centre, so in some ways it was similar to Coventry. Sadly it could be quite grim at times, especially when the weather was bad. They reckoned on a drop of two degrees centigrade up there and I would not argue with that. We were told dramatic stories of snow blizzards etc and people freezing to death, fortunately we were lucky for the four years we were there as the winters were quite mild.

The Church of England moved in almost from the beginning and rather interestingly it was the vicarage that was built first. The church of St. Clare was to follow a few years later and I shall always have a soft spot for this lovely Saint to whom St. Francis always went for a consultation before making any important decision. For those interested in such matters, she is the patron saint of television. The church was invariably locked up for much of the time, but at least there were daily services, and if you knew where a special access was, you could always get in for private prayer. The founding vicar had been trained at Kelham Monastery and so there was a hint of a liturgical arch and at the apex was set a Celtic cross, upon which a light always shone. That cross is still an abiding memory for me to this day. Outside was a civic flag pole, but there was no cenotaph, because Newton Aycliffe did not exist until after the war. Having said that, there was a strong military presence in the town with two Territorial Army depots and service clubs for each of the three arms of military service. There were two more churches, each with a Franciscan flavour, starting with St. Francis at Horndale. This was based on a C of E aided junior school. The worshipping community had a small chapel with their own rooms attached but moved into the school hall for their main Sunday service. A curtain on the stage could be hauled back to display a main altar with suitable liturgical accoutrements. The third church was that of St. Elizabeth of Hungary at Woodham, which was an upwardly middle class area on the edge of town. The church was a joint venture with the local community and was built on the end of the community centre. Remarkably, all this took place during the long interregnum when my three colleagues were manfully holding the fort. But perhaps I should now introduce my colleagues.

Daveth had taken a natural lead and was very much a charismatic priest in the best sense of the term. He came from Birmingham and had been trained at Cuddesdon, which meant that he was orthodox in matters theological. He was absolutely great with children and a gifted preacher. It was a great sadness in years to come when he decided that he must swim the Tiber. Then there was Frank who had a superb command of the Queen's English and went on during my time to obtain a doctorate. He had been a Company of Mission priest in a very rough parish closer to Durham. Frank could always be relied upon to explain difficult issues, especially to a recalcitrant PCC; he was also very, very courteous and extremely charming. Last, but not least there was Anne, who was a deaconess. She was extremely "catholic" and could be relied upon to keep us all in order. Within a few weeks of me arriving she was ordained deacon and that was a wonderful occasion. Anne was a widow and lived in a council house just the other side of the road to the vicarage. She became a very good friend and on Saturday night she would come across and join Hilary and me for drinks and nibbles. She was great fun and a loyal colleague. I must confess I had thought that she would swim the Tiber, but infact she decided to stay in and become ordained. She is a team rector up in Gateshead now. I had hardly started when the diocese persuaded Daveth to take up the parish of Dunston just outside of Gateshead. Not an easy parish by any means, but it did have a brewery! Incidentally he had also had a look at St. Luke's Holbrooks in Coventry before making up his mind.

This meant starting the whole process of interviewing again, which quite honestly, I could have done without. Eventually, Leon arrived from the other end of the Development Corporation in Peterlee. He was an American citizen who had married a local girl. He combined both a Geordie and an American accent – beat that if you will! Bishop Michael of Jarrow who was a monk and a first rate suffragan bishop thought that Leon needed a move and that he would get on much better with me than with his current incumbent. I think it was felt that I was more laid back and somewhat gentler and in addition would be happy to let Leon get on with things in his own way without constant interference. That was generally to be the case and I was particularly fortunate, since having taken Bill Hurworth the diocesan secretary out for a good lunch at my expense, he phoned me to say that I could go out and buy a four bedroomed house for Leon and his family. Money well spent. I would always recommend any new incumbent doing the same thing. It usually works wonders.

The day of my collation and institution arrived and a coach load came up from Shottery. I think that many of them actually wanted to both hear and see the "famous Bishop". They were not to be disappointed. The coach party had divided up, with some staying in comparative luxury at the Eden Arms and another group kipping down on the church hall floor and then there were those who made it as a one day trip. The weather was cold, but we were all warmed up by a rumbustious sermon from Bishop David. After the service there was the usual bun fight with gallons of tea. The wardens had said that the tradition was for there to be limitless tea, but did confess to knowing that most of the regulars would then go across the road to the pub or club. Shottery parishioners were highly delighted with the episcopal performance and, in fairness with the message. Bishop David stayed on for a long time and thoroughly enjoyed himself. His Brummie driver commented most favourably on the occasion, even if he found it difficult to smile. Bishop David met and spoke to Bishop John Daly who had served his first curacy at Tynedock and Archdeacon Derek met up again with my former boss, Father Tony Rowe. They had been at theological college together all those years ago and not met since. All in all a very happy occasion, and so next morning I celebrated the Holy Eucharist for the first time and Shottery saw what a High Church was like. We all then went out to lunch together and needless to say we chose a pub with a very definite railway connection. It was called "The Locomotion" and was situate at the station where the famous locomotive was put on the rails for the first time in September 1825. All that was needed was for the loco to be driven up to Shildon for the grand opening. For a loco to move you need steam, and for steam you need fire. Slight problem, because nobody had remembered to bring any matches! So, some enterprising individual got hold of a piece of glass and was able to re-direct the rays of the sun onto combustible material and, hey presto, as they say, the rest is history. The pub was good value, good real ale, good food, lots of railway and signalling artefacts and as an added bonus; the landlord was a former mainline driver. A most auspicious start. When we got home, it was decided to take the boys out for a walk and while we were out, my father-in-law got the shock of his life when the door bell rang and a monk appeared. It was just Bishop Michael enquiring as to whether we were all in good shape. I have to say that the pastoral concern by the diocese was first rate.

So, it was down to work and the first matter that needed my attention was the organ at St. Clare's. As my colleagues had said to me, I needed to be making decisions and be seen to be making decisions. The archdeacon had said quite rightly that the temporary organ had been put in without a faculty and this must be addressed as a matter of urgency. I had given him an undertaking that I would fully abide by the faculty jurisdiction procedures and not give him any hassle in that respect. He immediately became a good supporter of St. Clare's. We had been involved in a very gentle clash a few days previously when he put it to me that when I made by declaration of canonical obedience to the bishop and that I would do all things according to the book, that I might be breaking that promise by celebrating the service of benediction. I remember the very enquiring glance he made in my direction and my reply was quite simple. Yes. I agreed with him about the legality or otherwise of what he was saying, but presumably the diocese would apply the same approach to all the evangelical churches that used unauthorised family services? He saw my point, and nothing else was said on the subject. Fortunately for me, both my wardens were very keen on benediction. So, back to the organ. We had a meeting with the organ advisor, who clearly felt we should put in a pipe organ as being an object of beauty. My choir master, who was also a magistrate did not agree and went for him. I had to break them up. What we wanted was a quality electronic organ that would be so much cheaper for a relatively poor parish to manage. The matter went to the DAC who would not give an opinion, the archdeacon put in a most supportive letter, and the chancellor granted the faculty. That was a feather in all of our caps.

The next matter was for me to start the process of creating a team ministry and for a few months this involved me going round the diocese and talking to lots of different clergy. This was basically my remit for my time at Newton Aycliffe and I envisaged that it would take about four years. I was eventually proved to be correct. I also needed to consult with my colleagues and what we used to do was to go off for a day to the Convent of the Holy Rood in Thirsk. It was a delightful place and I retain happy memories to this day; unfortunately, the community no longer exists, as the sisters made a corporate decision to request dispensation from their vows. We would arrive in time for coffee, have a snooze and then go into town for a Pub lunch, then back to the convent for a plenary session in the afternoon. We joined the sisters for their evening office and then back into the real world.

Our family was about to increase as Hilary had arrived in County Durham, carrying our third child. Stephen David was born in Bishop Auckland on Good Friday 1987. The place of birth entitles him to be called a Wearsider. But being born on Good Friday was most inconsiderate. I had a phone call in the early hours of the morning to invite me to go in and meet my new son. It was a wonderful experience as I drove down the hill to Eldon, I could see all the lights of Bishop Auckland and Crook Town, and in the distance I could make out villages on the outliers of the Pennines. As I went in to to see Hilary on the ward, she greeted me with these words, "Hard luck mate, I am closing the innings!" I had wanted a girl, but Hilary had decided that she was not having any more of it. I went home and decided to say the daily morning office for Good Friday. I will always remember it, because the old testament lesson was from Genesis about the sacrifice of Isaac; who was I to complain? Then the milkman came to make his delivery and saw me sitting in the study, he almost dropped the bottles in shock. We brought Stephen home to the vicarage on Easter Sunday. Memorable! Stephen was in church on Low Sunday and everyone cooed over him, on more than one occasion, some of the locals came and crossed Hilary's hand with silver.

Hilary, like me did not find it easy to assimilate the local culture, and the boys had problems in that respect at school. The teachers commented on that fact on more than one occasion. Everything is so different. The currency might be the same, but that is where similarities finish. The lingo is different and the culture is totally different. An air of hopelessness pervaded everything and apathy was rife. Where we lived in the town centre was known as "Ation Corner", which stood for aggravation, intoxication and fornication, and there was evidence of all three activities in the bushes when I went to celebrate mass on the Sunday morning. It was also the scene of theft, because I was told that on the visit of the Queen, some years previously, a local had nicked the Royal Standard. Almost the same happened on the night of my induction because the flag of the bishop had disappeared and somebody had sprayed graffiti on the wall of the vicarage! And yet, it is so easy to criticise. Unemployment was rife and there were big queues at the dole House, the pubs and also the post office. Smoking was totally institutionalised and most of the funerals that I took were of people about ten years younger than would have been the case back in Shottery. This was still a proud community even if it was down and not quite out. They had a glorious military tradition to recall with pride. Most of the men had served in the Durham Light Infantry. It was said that there had only been two choices in life, and both involved the use of a spade. You either dug for coal, or you dug trenches to fight from. Many a wife, sister or daughter would wait agonisingly to know that their man had got back safe and well. If you are ever in Durham, it is well worth a look at the Durham Miners memorial in the cathedral. The Durhamites had this wonderful ability to cope and they were very enterprising in so many ways, but you could clearly see that there truly was a north/south divide.

One of the specialities was that of pilgrimage. There was an annual deanery pilgrimage which was always arranged by my colleagues. The first year we went to Whitby Abbey and Leon celebrated at the point of the original high altar, we then adjourned to the town below and I gorged myself on shell fish at a local parlour. I was especially grateful that some of the ladies offered to look after "the bairns", thus giving me the chance to follow some of my parishioners into a licensed premise close to the railway station. There were also the pilgrimages to Lindisfarne in Northumberland. These were not to be missed. The coach would drop us on the causeway and we would wade through the low tide on the path of St. Cuthbert and come up on the beach to the sound of Northumbrian pipes. Absolutely magical. There was then a mass in the grounds of the ruined abbey. Mind you, great care was needed in crossing over as you had to abide by the warning signs and not go over, even if it looked safe. The tides up there moved with incredible speed. And then there were the pilgrimages to Walsingham organised by the parish. For many parishioners, this represented their annual holiday and on the week after the return, they would start putting money in the pot ready for next year. We invariably used a coach that was owned by one of our regulars who came to the 8.00am service. Unfortunately I discovered too late that they were only really fit for local school runs. There was only one year when the coach actually made it to Walsingham and on one famous occasion, the shrine had to completely re-arrange all the accommodation for their visitors because we were going to be very late. I am told that much prayer was offered in the Holy House that night. Mind you, we had recovered by the morning and set to on our spiritual devotions with a vengeance. By lunch time, we usually went off to Wells for a walk in the pinewoods and on one very foolish occasion I agreed to take a dip in the sea (March), but I did manage to arrange some sponsorship and handed over to a delighted treasurer about £100. Then it was back to the shrine for the evening procession around the streets or around the gardens. For the last two years I took Mark and Peter, which gave Hilary a break and the boys entered into the spirit of the occasion by carrying the acolytes' candles. They were worn out when they came home and slept like logs.

We started to become more involved in local matters. Hilary decided to start up the very first Rainbow unit in the southern part of County Durham. It was a great success and big names from the Guiding hierarchy turned up for the first meeting. Not to be out done, I joined the scouts and started up a Beaver Colony which also met in the church hall. But very soon I was enticed into being a school governor, and was quickly voted in as Chairman of three Schools! Crazy, but that is what happened. On the first week of taking the chair at the big comprehensive school in town I was given two disciplinary files to read through. One related to a rape and the other to an attempted knife attack. This was really getting my hands dirty. But what irritated me was that the local councillors would do the rounds of the meetings, picking up £10 a time for a partial appearance and then go down to the club, and they did not want to hand over to any sub-committee. I needed to tackle this and fortunately for me, I had been seen down at the Legion Club by the political fixers in the town and the word went out round the manor that if I wanted anything like that, then nobody should vote against me. The first test was that of the appointment of the acting deputy assistant toilet cleaner for which a full governors' meeting had been called. I waded in and for the first time ever, the school had a subcommittee to deal with these very important matters. I then applied the same principle to the other schools and we managed to move on a bit.

Remembrance Sunday was taken very seriously, even though Newton Aycliffe had not existed during the war. It brought out the usual differences of opinion that you get in community life. The town clerk told me that when he first came to the town he had to lay down the law very firmly between the three military arms as to how things would be done and also as to the pecking order. I understand that on one occasion there was nearly an outbreak of World War III. What had happened was that after the appropriate ceremonies, the committee of the Royal British Legion branch had nabbed the saluting officer who actually was serving in the Royal Navy and whisked him off to the Legion club where he was suitably entertained and never got to the Royal Navy Club. It was therefore agreed that in future, all saluting officers would be taken over to the Legion Club for a drink and that if such saluting officer was serving in either the Royal Navy or the Royal Air Force, he would then be taken to the appropriate club for lunch. If the saluting officer was serving in the Army, then he would be taken either to the Officers' Mess at the R.E.M.E. Barracks or to the R.A.M.C. centre. This seemed to work and I spent some very convivial times there. Mind you it was very difficult to get to the bar, because the way was blocked by the town clerk and a very large police superintendent! Happy times.

It was clear to me that having our holiday break at Newton Aycliffe was a non starter. The day off was bad enough, so we looked for some affordable clerical holidays and started by going to our dearly loved Wells Next the Sea where there was accommodation for clerical families at Bishop Ingle House. This had been set up by a local lad who was eventually ordained and became bishop of one of the London episcopal areas. For a very modest fee you could take your family away for a week on full board. The manager was called Diana Lynch and the clergy did as they were told. Coffee was served in the drawing room and the children were banished to the nursery. On one famous occasion a good friend of mine who was a Canon of Durham Cathedral staggered in with a crate of red wine; Diana did not know where to put herself. We particularly enjoyed going over to Wells because we could go and see my godmother in Fakenham and visit the market with the sound of that glorious Norfolk accent. My godmother had married into the Aldiss family who were big landowners in mid Norfolk and when Diana found out, I suddenly realised that I had risen rapidly up the ranks of the local social hierarchy.

We also tried out Tranquillity House in Torquay. This had been set up by the tobacco barons just after the war to salve their consciences (well, that was the rumour anyway). The manager was called Mrs. Bishop and the full time assistant was called Miss Rosemary Sage. True! There was more than a hint of Barchester at Tranquillity House, but we had a great time there even having a night out by ourselves thanks to the kindness of a couple who agreed to babysit for us. It was all very formal, and grace was said at the beginning of each meal which was served up by Mrs. Bishop. Unfortunately the terms of the trust deed were very restrictive and did not allow for single priests to arrange a holiday for their housekeeper, even if that housekeeper was the priest's mother, which happened on more than one occasion.

Other holidays were taken up in Northumberland near to Alnwick with its glorious coastline where we inspected many a rock pool. Even at that time the local village churches were only having one service each month and seemed to be fairly happy with the situation. One Summer I decided to take our annual holiday in Scotland and do some parish duty on the Strontian Peninsula. It rained and rained and rained, so without waiting for the midges we decided to abort the holiday and go back south.

Chapter 11

NEWTON AYCLIFFE CONTINUED

It is worth telling a few gentle stories about the two bishops. They were both great value and yet very different. Bishop David may well have been famous for his academic prowess, but Bishop Michael could more than match him. There is still the story going around today that the cause of the great fire at York Minster just after the consecration of Bp. David was due to the divine displeasure of his theology. I have to tell you that it was the divine displeasure that the Faculty Jurisdiction Measure was now to be applied to cathedral as well as to parish churches. I had hardly settled in when a familiar coloured envelope dropped through the door. It was from Bp. David and out dropped a cheque for £400, which was serious money indeed. What he said was that he had received a block grant from the Church Commissioners to support parishes and clergy who were struggling in very difficult circumstances. He had no problem in saying that I was clearly one of those clergy. I have to say, that I was much gratified, especially as I had taken a pay cut of about £500 per annum for the privilege of going to the northeast. He was also very happy to support any initiatives that related to the community and readily agreed to open a Real Ale Festival for me. Then there was Bishop Michael, the monk. Like Bp David, Bp Michael was pastorally first rate. He was beloved by vicars' wives throughout the diocese as he had this habit (please excuse the pun) of knocking on the back door as he made a pastoral call and asking for a coffee. He then did the washing up if there was any left over from a previous meal. He was also an expert laundryman and when he was translated to Truro Diocese, they wheeled a twin tub washing machine into the cathedral as part of his leaving present. I valued his perception above all and often went to see him about having new curates when my colleagues moved on to other pastures. He would sit on his settee and look out of the window while conducting a conversation with me. Then would come the killer blow, "And what do you think, David?" As he turned around to face me, before returning to his original position. He always called me David, Bishop David called me Father David and when the archdeacon referred to me, I was always Mr. Capron!

Back to parish life. We had a very big Mothers' Union branch which was presided over by an eighty year old retired former headteacher. Gran Stout always carried a cane and would strike it hard onto the top of the table to obtain unquestioning silence; she would then say in a loud voice, "Ladies, the Vicar would like to address you." She would then turn to me and say, "Vicar, please address the meeting." We all knew where we stood. She was a first rate Christian lady and always said the evening office of compline before retiring to bed. She came to Newton Aycliffe with quite a reputation, having been headteacher of Horden Colliery Primary School. Those were the days when small communities were governed by certain ex-officio individuals, such as the vicar, the manager of the Co-op, the village policeman and the Head Teacher. The church tradition was Anglo catholic and so it was High Mass most Sundays with the branch secretary of the N.U.M. being the sub deacon, the thurifer was probably the pit deputy and the master of ceremonies would have been the miner in charge of the winding gear. To be part of these proceedings was considered to be a great honour and a privilege. Bishop Michael told me that if you had been down the pit all week, then the last thing you wanted was someone in a black gown, preaching at you. Much better to have colour, ceremonial, with some mystery and actually be involved. I have always remembered that, but then I was an Anglo catholic beforehand. Incidentally we only had incense at St. Clare's when we had monthly benediction, whereas the daughter church of St. Francis had it every Sunday. I know the archdeacon was not a big lover of it but he would back us to the hilt if anyone criticised us.

We were very lucky with babysitters as one family basically took over this problem for us. Pam and her two daughters were wonderful in just popping round for a few minutes or hours to help out. It was a great joy when for my very last wedding it was Pam's eldest daughter, Helen, who was the bride. Pam is now the Leader of the Mothers' Union, but she does not operate quite like Gran Stout. Pam is also a licensed pastoral assistant and so is very active in the parish as well as looking after grandchildren. We were especially grateful to her husband Michael, for introducing our two eldest boys to the joys of coarse fishing and they really took to it. There was so much free water in the town, that it was a cheap hobby to pursue and clearly gave some sort of release to the many men who were on the dole. Michael fished at the very highest levels and his name could be found frequently in the Angling Times. He even influenced me, but it took a few more years before I took it up again, although admittedly on a much reduced basis.

I got myself involved with the great oval ball game and became secretary of the local rugby club. Incidentally it is the Union code in County Durham and not league. I think many of the lads had a bit of a culture shock in reverse, because I did not really fit their traditional idea of a vicar. I did manage to infiltrate the high echelons of the county rugby authorities by fixing it for one of my players who had been sent off to be immediately re-instated. There were some ribald comments when the matter came up for discussion, but basically, I decided to dress up with all the gear and play the part of a deferential secretary. So I arrived with rolled brolly, executive brief case, ecclesiastical specs, three piece suit with watch and chain. The committee thought that I was some joker who had come in fancy dress and were about to throw me out when I said that I would pray for them and they realised that I was not just the local poser. I must confess that I did rather play it out by agreeing that it had been the sort of game where invariably there was going to be a sending off and, of course, that the ref had handled the game extremely well. When asked for my overall view as to the correctness of the dismissal, I posited the thought that perhaps in this one particular circumstance, there might be some merit in allowing the appeal, without undermining the disciplinary procedures. I won that one, but a few weeks later my member was sent off again and so I told him that he was on his own!

The railway heritage of the area gave me the opportunity to spend some time with Mark and Peter and introduce them to the delights of train-spotting with the added bonus for Hilary that she could have some time just with Stephen. However before we eventually moved down south, I was able to take all three out on a trip to Hull, complete with potty which was soon needed as our 156 class DEMU sped towards the Humber estuary. But our favourite spot was Darlington Bank Top which we used to visit most Friday evenings and be amused by the porters who used to take the boys on trips aboard their little platform scooters. There were always plenty of trains and if you stood down at the London end of the Up platform, then it was a joy to behold. By this time the 125s, were reigning supreme and they are still going to this day. Then there were the little 142s and 144s which pootled along between Saltburn and Bishop Auckland. I remember taking my Beaver colony to the station for one of our gatherings and actually installing one or two of them with the Scout promise etc. Despite being in the heart of railway country, many of them had never been on a train at all, but they all remembered the very long ticket that the guard had to print out from his machine to cover about twenty four Beavers and four or five adults. The next best place to see the trains was to perch ourselves on the fence at Aycliffe village and see the big beasties rush through at tremendous speed. And last but not least I could always wander down the now defunct Clarence Railway embankment and dream about the electric railway of yesteryear.

We had by now been in Aycliffe for three years and I could begin to see the end of my time there. The team ministry had been set up by order in council which meant that on one particular night I went to bed as a vicar and woke up as a rector. It was quite painless, I hasten to add. But also, my colleagues were all going off to pastures new. There had been no fall out, but quite literally they had done their time and should move on. Doctor Frank took up some parishes in the depths of rural Northants, Anne went to Eldon which was almost next door and Leon eventually went to York as a Vicar Choral in the cathedral. So for the last year, I was totally by myself. It was not long after this happened that we went as a family for a trip up the Wear Valley Railway on a Sunday special to Stanhope. When the train pulled into Witton le Wear, a priest got on, who I recognised, together with a walking party from his parish. We exchanged pleasantries and the next thing that happened was that he got up and made a speech. What he said in public for all on the train to hear was to introduce me and then to slate the Diocese of Durham for leaving me by myself in a parish of 30,000 souls. I must confess that I was flabbergasted, but at least he got off at Frosterley and I was spared any further embarrassment. We arrived at Stanhope and the driver and guard suggested that we all take our families down to the playing fields for the next half hour. It was great fun, but since our trip up the dale I have learned that Stanhope was notorious as the richest benefice in the Church of England. So rich in fact, that when its vicar went to be Bishop of Exeter, he wanted to hang on to the living because he just could not exist on the paltry pay that he would receive as a bishop. Makes you think, doesn't it? Mind you, this scenario was the basis of that trollopian character, Dr. Vesey Stanhope, the residentiary canon of the cathedral at Barchester who spent most of his time in Italy collecting butterflies. To bring us back to the present, after a while the guard and driver suggested that we all make our way back to the train ready for the return journey.

Managing a parish in the circumstances already described was not exactly easy, and so I was very grateful for the offer from my neighbour at Shildon to send his curate to cover the 9.30am mass at St. Francis, Horndale. Baptisms were almost impossible to sort out as we did a roaring trade in that respect. Needs must, so I resorted to very basic tactics. We had an open surgery in the choir vestry and all I could do was to put three boxes on the table with application forms adjacent and then a big map of the town divided up into three pastoral areas. There was a further notice which invited applicants to consult the map so as to establish which area they lived in, then to look at the other lists and find out when the actual services were going to take place. Forms were then completed and put in the appropriate box; after that, all they had to do was to turn up. Not very satisfactory, but I had no alternative and despite requests further up the chain for a ruling, nothing came down. There were mutters of course, but I was not in any mood to be more accommodating. Someone was heard to say that he was not having his kid baptised in a b— school hall, so I told him straight that if he didn't like it then he would not have his b— kid baptised at all! And yet there were funny sides to this problem as the undertakers decide to move into the town and the parlour was manned by Hilda who was the deputy warden at St. Francis. This resulted in the funeral parlour being the place to go to fix hatching, matching as well as dispatching. I think the theology is perfect.

Hilary and I had always reckoned that we would go back south and I was glad for support from both bishops who said that I had done the job required of me and whenever I might go, I would do so with their blessing. So the search was on and I put myself on various lists which necessitated going down to London. At least I can always say that I have crossed the portals of No. 10 Downing Street as I went to see the ecclesiastical appointments adviser to the Prime Minister. Great feeling as I walked up the road that cabinet ministers tread, but there was not much on offer other than a grotty combination of parishes on south Humberside, which I promptly turned down. I did go and look at another parish south of Scunthorpe, but although it was quite pleasant, I did not think that there would be enough there to keep me occupied. Then there was the offer of a cluster of village churches in the heart of the Cotswolds, which on the face of it looked absolutely fabulous. However, from what I could see, it could only justify about three days at the most per week and I enquired if there was a diocesan appointment that could be coupled with it? By the time that a reply was ready to come back, the diocese of Gloucester contacted me urgently with copious apologies as a former parish priest who had gone abroad on missionary duties had returned in desperate need of a gentle parish. No contest. Then I had a phone call from a very old friend of mine at Arrow – Chris Baker. We had boarded together at Rugby and knew each other well. The message was that Alan Shaw, the Rector of Alcester and Arrow with Weethley had died and would I be interested? Do I hear you say, that Barchester rules? Well, at least the Rector had died and there was not the rather unsavoury business of not being sure of how to actually pray at the bedside. So, in some ways, the rest is what they call, history, but there was still quite a lot to do up north before coming back south.

To cut a long story short, I came back down to Coventry diocese to renew my acquaintance with Bishop Simon. We knew each other from the very first days of his episcopal ministry and I particularly remember his enthronement on the vigil of the Epiphany 1986 when it snowed, and boy, did it snow! He had then started his tour of the deaneries and had celebrated his visit to the Fosse Deanery by coming to Shottery. After the initial pleasantries, it was agreed that I should meet up with the parish representatives. Note, there had been a change and it was not necessarily the wardens. So I met up with Michael and Andrew, although the meeting did not go as well as it might have. I knew rather a lot about Alcester, in fact I knew much more than the parish realised, so when the diocese did not send any paperwork with me, they were rather left in the lurch. When this little problem had been cleared up, everything fell into place and the formal offer came through. I now needed to tell Newton Aycliffe and prepare for the move.

Bishop Michael told me that I must not feel guilty about leaving. He told me that I would be accused of letting them down – and I was – but, as he told me later, they said the same to everyone! Still, there were still some very pleasant things to do. I had carried out a carol service at the local R.A.M.C. depot and so Hilary and I were invited to a cocktail party in the officers Mess. This sort of thing was a rare event indeed. When we arrived we were greeted with jugs. Lots and lots of jugs which were all brimming with gin and tonic! Fortunately we were well within walking distance, so there was not a problem in that respect. Being the army, we were well looked after and the evening proceeded apace. Then, after about an hour the Commanding Officer said in a very loud voice, "Ladies and Gentlemen, The Band Sergeant Major." And everyone got up! There was much military guffawing and then we all sat down again to enjoy the rest of the evening. At the other end of the scale I remember having a drink in the Legion Club and there was a very miserable looking guy next to me who suddenly got up and marched to the bar for a refill. He then about turned and marched back. I enquired of a friend as to why this chap was so miserable and was told in all sincerity that drinking was a serious business.

I know that there has not been much theology in these two chapters, but I would suggest that there is rather more than might at first be apparent. I needed to get involved and get around. I also needed to say my prayers and either celebrate or attend mass each day. This was my spiritual diet and without it, even if it looked and felt watery, it was absolutely fundamental and I could not have exercised a priestly ministry. When I was by myself, the best way to get away was to go up onto the hills above Hamsterley Forest which is an outlier of the Pennines. We also used to go up as a family and it was ideal for my Beaver colony as I could negotiate a preferential rate with my eight o'clocker for the relatively short coach trip. I remember on one occasion disturbing a red deer which crashed out of the bushes and then there was the red squirrel which was an absolute joy to behold. Our faithful dog, Honey had a wonderful time sniffing at everything that could be sniffed and joy of joys there was the river which meant we all got very wet.

We now started to sort out a date for the move and also schools in Alcester, which fortunately proved to be very straightforward. It was decided that we would move south on August 1st 1990 with licensing towards the end of September. Bishop David was happy for me to have a break and keep me on the payroll, so to speak. Without appearing to be unnecessarily mean, it would be a big rise in stipend. Many people have no idea what life was and still is like up there. We sit in our warm and comfortable homes and moan about any changes around us that we do not like but it would do people in south Warwickshire good to go up to somewhere like Newton Aycliffe. It is a proud county, they served their country with distinction in the world wars; you only have to look at the number of battalions raised under the banner of the Durham Light Infantry. They also work and they work very hard, they have no time for laziness. It is just that for so many reasons beyond their power, they have drawn the short straw every single time. I know what it is like to want to work and to find that there is no work about. The communities in Durham are from what you might term to be on the whole, the right wing of the labour party. The co-operative movement which in many ways was and still is the height of respectability. Big union men and women they certainly are, but they had no time for Arthur Scargill when he spoke at the Durham Miners Gala. He went on at length about nuclear disarmament and was never invited again!

So, we had to start the process of saying goodbye once again. Yes we did make good friends and we are still in touch to this day. I am so glad that we did go up to the Kingdom of Northumbria, but I am also glad that we came back to the Kingdom of Mercia. I will always speak up for my former parishioners and for the northeast in general. Admittedly south Durham is different to Newcastle and I well remember being told after my licensing at Alcester by a new parishioner who came originally from Consett that there was a difference and not to forget it. His accent was not far off being pure Geordie.

So we had our last service in St. Clare's and I said goodbye to that Celtic cross which had always inspired me. Then it was a faith supper and the inevitable speeches. I am still sure to this very day that Newton Aycliffe could never get their head around a Public School boy from the affluent south of England coming up to spend time with them and share a bit of his life with them. I am so glad that I did and have no regrets, because at the end of the day, there is always a greater purpose and our time at Alcester was to prove very fulfilling.

The remover's vehicles arrived and everything was packed up. It was stinking hot and I was not really looking forward to the drive south. It certainly proved to be difficult and the boys became somewhat fractious, which meant that I got ratty, leaving Hilary to keep the peace and for Honey to look very bemused. As we drove out for the last time and drove under the bridge of the old Clarence Railway I honked the horn vigorously and we were finally on our way.

Chapter 12

THE MOVE ONTO THE GREVILLE ROAD ESTATE CALLED LES TRIANONS!

If you are wondering what Les Trianons means, then I will tell you. They were very high class and extremely intimate houses provided by the Kings of France for their mistresses at Versailles. Mind you when we saw the furnishings and fittings which had been left to us by the builders in what had previously been the show house, we began to wonder, as the main bedroom was kitted out in a very definite horseriding mode.

It was very hot and so I popped down to Gateway, as it was in those days to buy a few necessities and bumped into Maurice Savage the warden from Weethley, so we had a brief chat and, as I turned to walk back to the car, I could not believe what I saw in front of me. It was a very large HGV all the way from Newton Aycliffe. I went up to the driver and told him that I was his vicar. He did not seem very impressed. Once I got home, there was no sign of the boys as they had soon disappeared to play with a host of other children on the estate. We were mightily relieved and got on with the job of unpacking. It was a very pleasant week and we put our respective parents to work which kept them occupied, leaving us to do other things. A few days later I decided to slink round to the Roebuck for a quiet pint, thinking that nobody would know me. No such luck! "How is the Vicar of Shottery?" asked Dick Goode the landlord. Then I remembered that I had done much business with the Goode family when I was at Shottery. By which I mean, "hatching, matching and dispatching". Unfortunately it wasn't long before there was a big fire and substantial damage which entailed a lengthy period of repair. As so often happens on these sorts of occasions, the landlord was at another pub in the town having a drink with all the other landlords.

We had not been ensconced all that long when I had a call from a delegation of the Royal British Legion. If I remember rightly, it was Peter

Robinson and John Buchanan. They were absolutely charming and we went down the road for a drink together as they wanted to establish that I was happy to go along with their normal Remembrance Day Festival arrangements. No problem at all, and I suspect that in any case, word had come down from the northeast that I could be relied upon to play a straight bat. However I did need to make one or two changes, as I looked at the service sheet which they had been using and was far from happy as it did not look at all like what I was used to. I rang up Mary Beattie who had been my secretary in Newton Aycliffe and asked her to post me a copy of what we had used up there. Clearly, what had happened in Alcester was that a form of service had been knocked up in the past and nobody felt that they could change it, so change it, I did. It ended up as being basically the same as that used at the Cenotaph in London for the outside act of remembrance! I also nipped up to pay my respects to the Patron of the Living, Hugh Seymour, 8th Marquess of Hertford. He was good fun and we got on very well, I also knew that he had served in Suez with the Grenadier Guards and so I felt I could ask for approval of the new draft service. All he asked for was that we might have the hymn, "O Valiant Hearts" I certainly was not going to argue that point and we have had it ever since. There were some comments from the committee that the service order had changed, but my point that it was now virtually the same as in London, coupled with fulsome support from the Lord of the Manor, meant that there no more mutters. The service went like a bomb and I experienced the view of the Lord of the Manor leading his troops up the High Street with bowler and brolly! You could not really get that anywhere else but Alcester. After the service a few of the old soldiers came up to me and thanked me profusely for all the arrangements. "You got that right, Padre, and not too much glory either." Interesting! What would the politicians have said to that remark I wonder? I have other stories to tell in this respect later on in the book.

There were other personalities who needed attention in those early days and one of them was, my personal and self appointed secretary, Hilda Jones, also known as Daffy or Tilly, who had presided over a long list of rectors. Very traditional, high church and unquestionably loyal to her rector. The main problem was trying to take some work away from her so that others might have a chance and we could actually delegate and practice the basics of mutuality and interdependence; but it was difficult.

On the other hand, I could happily pass on much of the drudgery of administration to her and she lapped it up. What with her and Len Chambers who was the very traditional verger and still with us some twenty years later, I really counted myself as being very lucky indeed. Len has hung up his vergers rod, but still keeps his hand in even at the age of 95 years. Wonderful and I reckon that it is a combination of the air and water that affords long life in this old Roman town!

But perhaps a little could be said about Alcester. It is situate on a Roman road and at the confluence of two rivers. The ancient name is "Alauna" and it was a prosperous settlement for the first three centuries after the birth of Christ. There was a camp up on Oversley Hill which commanded a good view of the midland plain and also a potential attack route from the southwest. After a period of time the Romans upped sticks and went. Eventually, the area was civilised once again and it is rumoured that St. Chad visited Alcester as it had come to his notice that the behaviour of the locals left much to be desired. He arrived on his horse and remonstrated with them, but to no avail with the result that he was chased out of town and generally roughed up. Has anything changed? I ask myself. To cap it all, he put a curse on the town, which did not seem to work as the town has continued to prosper ever since. In later life, the town was known for malting, needles and agricultural produce. The big estates ensured an efficient form of production and especially that at Ragley. The town has a charter which is read out by the High Bailiff at the Annual Mop Fair, it is therefore, not a village. Studley may be slightly bigger, but it is a village! The Lord of the Manor was the boss. He appointed a Steward as his go between with the Court Leet in the town and it was the duty of the High Bailiff to ensure that the duties and taxes were all collected in and paid over. In addition, law and order was maintained and the quality of goods and services was ensured. The Court Leet has no legal powers nowadays, but retains an important ceremonial function for which I suspect our American cousins would die for. There are not many Court Leets left, but locally they can still be found at Henley in Arden and Bromsgrove with vestiges in Stratford upon Avon and Warwick. Needless to say, the most popular post on any Court Leet is always that of Ale Taster!

The day of my licensing arrived and I remember telling Hilary that she would need to sit in the Rector's wife's pew: front left with the Marquess and his family on the front right. The boys were much amused and the service went very well. I had walked across the fields to the sound of bells. I felt like Frank Kilvert of diary fame and after the service there was the inevitable bun fight down at the Greig Memorial Hall. My former parishioners from up northeast were mesmerised when they walked down Butter Street as Alcester is so different to Newton Aycliffe. Over those first few months I had to make some important decisions and also be seen to be consulting as there were still mutters as to how quickly my colourful predecessor had been appointed and put into office. Before Alan Shaw, there had been a much loved personality called Arthur Stally, whose ministry is still remembered with much affection. The sort of services was a pressing matter and what part any choir might take. I decided to ask the choir to return and to be prepared to sing a five part setting for a Sung Eucharist on all Sundays at 11.00am with the exception of the second Sunday when there had usually been a Family Service. There was also Choral Evensong and an eight o'clock Holy Communion. Alcester was clearly a fairly conventional place so I decided to use BCP at the eight o'clock and this went down very well as I also decided that the congregation would get a short sermon, even if it was only five minutes. Being of a catholic background I also decided that there would be an additional week day Eucharist on Tuesday evenings and eucharistic celebrations for all the saints days as prescribed by canon law. There would of course be variations at special times of the year. I also needed to provide for Arrow and Weethley. Arrow is the estate church of Ragley and is situate close to the River Arrow at the end of a track. The setting is sylvan to say the least and is graced by the adjacent old rectory which is now in private hands. It is even more conventional than Alcester with the formal seating for the great and good, additionally adorned with knobs for the gentlemen to hang their toppers. Hence the name, Big Knobs! An old boy who was around at the time could just remember the last time that the Seymour family vault was opened up at about the time of the First World War. He told us that four horses and block and tackle had been used to remove the concrete slab. Finally, there is the Chapel of Ease of St. James the Great up at Weethley. There is a small pond adjacent to the churchyard and on a very clear day you can just make out the Brecon Beacons. There are nearly always good views of the Malverns, the Cotswolds and just possibly a hint of the Quantocks Hills, but then as a Somerset man, you would expect me to say that!

Back to Alcester for a while. I had been given a list of weddings that were on the horizon and one was of particular interest because it was that of the Earl of Yarmouth who was the heir to the Marquisate. This gave me quite a lot of extra work and a hell of a lot of aggro, but not from this end, I hasten to say. The family had decided that the wedding should be on a Saturday evening just after the shops had closed for Christmas shopping. That decision meant that I had to apply for a Special Licence from the Faculty Office of the Archbishop of Canterbury and there was the problem. The fact that the bride was Brazilian and a Roman Catholic was delightfully straightforward. So I had to make the appropriate moves and talked to my old friend, David Dumbleton who warned me that the faculty office could be very awkward and that I would have to lay it on thick. So I did, but they did not like it and turned it down, as they said, they did not want to encourage such practices and in any case they did not want to be seen to bowing down to the aristocracy. I must confess that I thought the application was perfectly fair in the circumstances and that it would be very much an Alcester occasion, so I trotted off to see Bishop Simon who was most encouraging and said that he would deal with the matter, but that he would pray about it first. Well, after about a week, I reckoned that Bishop Simon had had enough time to pray and for the Almighty to be persuaded one way or the other. I went back to Bishop Simon and he took it up with a vengeance so that eventually those miserable characters, very grudgingly agreed to the request, but put down all sorts of conditions. In his letter, Bishop Simon had written as follows: "I know of no other parish where a market town is under the shadow of a kind of chateau in the almost Gaelic way in which Alcester relates to Ragley!" Immortal words indeed. Bishop Simon could certainly write a good letter and when we spoke again about this matter he very wickedly said that if there were any further problems, then he would just have a word with, "Robert". I must confess I was glad when all the legal bits were sorted out, because the last thing I wanted was for questions to be asked in the House of Lords.

But before that particular wedding, another one took place but in very dramatic circumstances. The week before, it snowed and it snowed and it snowed. The boys were delighted and Honey had a whale of a time jumping in and out of snow drifts. You could hardly move and I only just managed to walk into town to say the morning office and get the paper. It froze and it froze, so that it was dangerous to even attempt to drive and I had a wedding on the Saturday morning. Hilary loaded me up with hot drinks and sarnies as I decided to walk in with my bag which also contained, cassock, change of shoes etc. I told her that I would be back of course, but could not guarantee a time and in any case there were power cuts everywhere. When I arrived at St. Nicks I was greeted by Len who told me that there was no heat. There was also no power in the bell chamber which meant that the bells could not be rung as there was no emergency backup. A good start indeed, then the casualties started as follows. The parents of the groom were turned back by the police at Oxford, the groom ended up in a hedge on his way here from Stratford and only 25 guests turned up. I kept in regular contact with the mother of the bride and told her that we would have to wait for the groom in any case, but also that it was freezing in church, but we could go ahead if she wanted. I was told that mother wanted her daughter married. I therefore waited for the groom who eventually turned up, not any the worse, and then phoned the bride's mother. We agreed to start in half an hour, so I then went round to see the choirmaster, Richard Dobell who was dispensing generous libations of brandy to the choir and said that the wedding was now definitely "on". It took place and is remembered best by me for the superb rendering by Richard of the famous, "Widor" on the piano. It was a masterful performance of the highest calibre. I felt so sorry for the couple and offered them a repeat performance (subject to legality) free of charge, but they never came back to me on that.

And now there was the big one, so to speak and I needed to meet up with the happy couple. By this time the Roman Catholic Church had woken up to the fact that there was going to be a very high powered "mixed" marriage and the next thing that happened was that various faculties were issued telling the local priest, Father Aidan that another priest was being authorised to attend in his place. Father Aidan did not mind as he was invited to the reception and I remember him telling some first rate stories after he had been fortified with champagne. The visiting priest was Father Derek Jennings who was a chaplain at London University and clearly moved in high circles. His Eminence the Cardinal used to pop in for supper and Father Derek also knew the Ragley family very well, so it all looked good. We met before the wedding to discuss a few matters and agreed that other than the legal bit, we would split the service right down the middle. He also said that he needed to be seen by his superiors as playing a straight bat as to the religious education of any children and would I mind if he could say to his superiors that he would always be welcome in Alcester. I could see his problem and there was nothing for him to worry about. It was also interesting that, when out of earshot, he had no problem in saying that I was a validly ordained priest as far as he was concerned. Needless to say I warmed to him and it was tragic that within a few years he had died of cancer. The wedding was a great success and the party up on the hill was even more so. Hilary was really looking forward to the whole event and at the dinner found herself sitting amongst a varied collection of the English and foreign aristocracy. There were six Dukes including H.R.H. the Duke of Kent, the godfather of the groom. It was good to meet him and he came into the Lady Chapel to sign as a witness. What some of you may not realise is that when members of the aristocracy append their signature, they just use their title. So we had on the wedding registers the following: Hertford, Yarmouth, Kent. The finale was quite dramatic as Lady Louise, the Marchioness, had intended that the happy couple would depart before midnight. Hints of Cinderella do I hear you say? Well, there was a big rush when it was seen what the time was and so Lord Harry and Beatriz his new wife were encouraged to leave before the clock struck with the result that Lord Harry drove his car into that belonging to the Steward of the Manor and there was much chuckling from the Big House as we slowly brought the social proceedings to an end. But now, it is time to come down from the hill in the spirit of the Transfiguration!

I started a long association with what was then called St. Faith's School, by going in to take a weekly assembly and also getting involved with rugby practice. Those were happy times indeed as the two eldest boys had started there and Hilary was to become increasingly involved over the years. There was a degree of conventionality, which was appropriate to Alcester and in the past there had been the suggestions that the School had not pushed its pupils enough, but that was now something of the past and the School prospered. There was much mirth when a visiting choir came from Germany to perform for the school. First of all they had to be persuaded to extinguish their cigarettes before entering and then were amazed to see the local children all spick and span in their uniforms. I soon learned that the Germans had basically got rid of uniforms after the war. But there was more to come, because they naturally thought that the German language would not be used, but were flabbergasted when one of the class teachers who had been born in Germany, addressed them all in impeccable German. It was a good opportunity for some of the local children to make a return trip and it did not take very long for Peter and then Stephen to cash in on that opportunity. Grateful thanks to that very charismatic deputy head, Mick Perrier for arranging those choral and cultural exchanges.

We knew that we would not be at Greville Road for too long as the Diocese was determined that we should live in the centre of the town. This meant applying for planning permission and carrying out much legal work in preparation as well as talking to concerned neighbours. The diocese had started on a plan to completely renew the parsonage stock in the diocese and if this meant selling old rectories and building new ones, then so be it. Some of the locals did not see it that way and quite a few objections were registered including one from the town council and as is the norm in these sorts of situations the district council refused permission and the diocese sat down to lick its wounds. But it did not take long for them to decide that they were not going to let this go and employed the services of a planning consultant, and for a while, everything went quiet.

We had more than enough to do and Hilary soon decided that she was going to start up a Rainbow unit to add to local Guiding. Before long she took on the role of district commissioner and renewed links with Guiders in Stratford as well as the Trefoil Guild. I must have attended hundreds of meetings in those early years and of course there were always the annual meetings to keep you interested. My first at Alcester turned out to be quite dramatic because Bill Roberts who was the licensed Reader for the benefice had a heart attack just before evensong which was going to precede the APCM. I spoke to Michael and Ken and said that I should be with Bill and his family. This was agreed and I left them to sort out evensong and look after the meeting while I went up to Redditch Hospital to see Bill. Fortunately it was not quite as bad as we thought and eventually he was back on his feet and we breathed freely again. Bill was the former Police Sergeant who had lived in the town for some years. He was Steward of the Manor of Alcester and was involved with just about everything that went on. I think that if you had put Hilda and Len with Bill, then there would not have been much left that they were not involved with. In many ways the most important work that Bill did was that relating to the various charities. He was clerk to all of them and told me that I was now ex officio a member of the Moorfields and United Charities, plus some other small ones that have since been wound up. The Moorfields was set up for the benefit of the inhabitants of Alcester, but with a special desire that the maintenance of the fabric of the established church should take first place in our deliberations. The United Charity dealt with six almshouses on the Birmingham Road plus an educational trust and a small one that looked after the poor.

The planning application ground on and we forgot about it as other more pressing matters came to our attention. We soon had to sort out further education for Mark and ultimately for both Peter and Stephen. We were therefore highly delighted when they were accepted at St. Benedict's R.C. School in Alcester. There began a long and very happy relationship with that school and it was not long before I found myself as one of the governors there, as well as, of course, at St. Faith's. Stephen was now big enough to go to school and so we sent him to Alcester Infants which was a feeder school to St. Faith's. Mark and Peter got involved with Cubs and Scouts and it was not long before Stephen joined my Beaver colony. One day, I had a phone call from John Allen the Diocesan Secretary who I knew was a keen bell ringer. All he wanted was permission for a team of bell ringers from Lichfield cathedral to ring our bells which had a good reputation. No problem I said and passed the message on to the captain of the tower so that they could be welcomed. They had a good time, made very complimentary remarks about the quality of the Alcester bells, stuffed a lot of money into the bell rope fund box and then went down the pub. Later, they turned up at Bidford to ring the bells there and were greeted with incredulity when the Bidford ringers found out that the visitors had been at Alcester. It turned out that Bidford had wanted to go there for years!

I had another phone call from John Allen on the matter of planning and he was absolutely jubilant as the appeal against refusal had been heard and upheld. He was in seventh heaven and if I had asked for a Jacuzzi to be added to the house, then I am sure I would have got it. Despite a little more skirmishing about the construction process, contracts were signed and work commenced in April 1994. In the meantime we had a delightful visitor in the person of Father Emmanuel from Ghana. I was on the Governing Body of the USPG Missionary College in Selly Oak at the time, so this was an excellent opportunity for us all to broaden our horizons. Emmanuel was Archdeacon of Cape Coast and when he went home he became the Dean of the Cathedral and ultimately Vicar General during the Episcopal interregnum. He is now Archdeacon of Saltponds which is a missionary area in the centre of the diocese and we keep in regular contact to this day. I think that many of us remember a particular sermon when he preached about Jesus being the son of a carpenter and that his father was also a carpenter! Emmanuel would be very quiet for a while but when he had something to say it was usually with tremendous exuberance, especially when watching a football match on the television. He looked very impressive and particularly so when wearing red vestments. We were sorry when he went back home. But he was to return a few years later with his wife Juliana and we soon renewed our friendship. He certainly brought in a breath of fresh air and commanded a great deal of respect.

But at last, work started on the new parsonage and the boys were fascinated, ensuring a visit every day so as to keep tabs on everything. Hilary and I are sure that it was this early attention to what was going on that got Peter on the path to what he is now – a chartered architect! While this was going on we had to make decisions as to colours of paint, some amendment to ensure that the outside area was covered over and that an adjacent en-suite was constructed next to our bedroom. Next we had to sort out the furnishings and eventually a day for the move which took place on November 2nd, 1994. The festival of All Souls. Little did I realise that in the years to come that date would be indelibly inscribed on my heart.

Chapter 13

THE SECOND MOVE AND THE SECOND LICENSING!

I took two weeks extra holiday so as to help out both in the house and in the garden. The boys had to decide which of their three bedrooms they wanted; needless to say, Stephen did not have much of a say in this particular respect. Mark chose the biggest and Peter got the one with the wash basin. There was also the opportunity of exploring up in the roof space and plans were soon afoot to install a model railway system. The first night that we had there was pleasantly interrupted by a knock at the door to find Andrew and Marion with a bottle of bubbly, so we invited them in and gave them a guided tour. We also had an open house evening when libations of all sorts simply flowed and flowed. We were delighted that the Marquess and Marchioness also joined the house warming party. Despite the encouraging start there were always going to be problems about right of access, both pedestrian and vehicular and it has now only fairly recently been substantively resolved. The family has a cut through from Butter Street for which we retain sets of keys, but we can drive up Old Rectory Garden without any problem. So, our first neighbours were Jean and Albert who lived in the vergers lodge. As I went past to go to church, the door was usually open and Albert would be sitting there, deciding on his daily investment for the horses. On one occasion when Jean was not about, he asked if I could nip down the "Offie" and buy him a half bottle of whisky. On my return, Jean had returned herself, but I still had a snifter. There were lots of advantages in now living in the centre of the town, such as it being far less distance for the boys to go to school, a short trip to get the newspaper and of course, so much closer to church that I began to virtually live there.

The whole question of what we should do in the church at Alcester now began to exercise the corporate mind of the PCC. Where had we come from? Where were we going? How were we going to get there? We had long discussions about our approach to mission. At the end of the day we were in business for the benefit of those who did not come to church. We therefore made two fundamentally very important decisions. First we needed to make the church both attractive and comfortable and secondly we needed to take the church out into the community. I have never been keen on churchy organisations and as a certain diocesan secretary, Simon Lloyd, has said to me, "Your Mission is where your feet are"! I reckon if you count up and make a list of all the organisations that exist in Alcester, then you are bound to find a goodly proportion of local Christians. The town is not so easy to work as at first thought, because you have to fight your corner, but at least the church is not looked at with indifference and we set to work with a vengeance to do a good job with baptisms, funerals and weddings. I want to say more about the occasional offices at the end of the book, but we soon had the laity actively involved and I have a lot to be thankful for to Marion and the Mothers' Union, Gill, Florence, Sheila and Jean who have all added that extra dimension to ministry with the result that the church is meaningful to the community that it serves.

But we did need to look after the fabric and to cut a long story short, we must have raised about £250,000 in those early days which covered repairing the whole of the tower, the lead on the roof, the front drive, the church wall, the internal lighting, the computerised heating system, internal decorations, floor tiling etc, etc. There were enthusiastic money raisers about and some incredible schemes were instituted that brought in the cash! The book stall was one of those. It had been set up by Kathleen Saunders who was a mathematics graduate from Oxford and a former principal of a teacher training college. Kathleen was a good friend to me, but we all knew where we stood. It did not take long before the nicknames started to appear and I went to the front of the queue with, "Auntie Wainwright", because you could not possibly leave before having made a purchase. She drove a hard bargain with her suppliers and invariably would not deal unless she was granted sale or return terms of business. I remember taking her to Worcester on one occasion when she went to the S.P.C.K. shop. We were virtually bowed in. The basket on wheels was left downstairs with the order list while we went out for afternoon tea. When we returned it had been carried upstairs, filled up with the requisite books and then brought downstairs again for our collection. Another nickname was, "She who is Mighty". Again, I must confess my guilt in this respect. When Kathleen was on duty at the stall, there was no doubt as to who was presiding. Quite a few of the ladies were scared stiff of her, but she was fine and once you knew how to play a type of game with her, then everything was OK. I remember during an early discussion making the point that the finances of the book stall must be under the ultimate control of the PCC. But, the treasurer still had to make his annual visit to extract the funds. It was all part of a game and we had great fun and now have wonderful memories.

My verger Len was full of vigour even then in his mid to late seventies. I put him up to be a recipient for the Maundy Money when her Majesty the Queen came to Coventry Cathedral. He got the shock of his life when the letter arrived and Doris was over the moon. It meant a lot to him and I was pleased that some recognition had gone his way. So, how could we recognise Hilda? This proved to be a little easier than we had anticipated because everything fell into place as we decided to hire the Town Hall and have a commemorative lunch with some old fashioned parish entertainment. This was provided by the Conway Trio who came out of retirement for this one and only performance. One of the members ended up as Chairman of the Bench and another one as Chairman of the District Council. In those early days they used to perform down at the Trades and Labour Club on the estate and are still remembered to this day. Anyway, Hilda went home, a very happy and still a very loyal lady.

During this time, there had been a change of wardens. Ken and Michael now hung up their staves to be succeeded by David and Sheila. They were as different as chalk and cheese which meant that it worked and worked well. It was then that prospective colleagues both ordained and licensed came to live in Alcester. Canon John Cooke will swear that it was a beaming Sheila who greeted him at the front door as he arrived to take a service for me that decided him and Daphne that they should make one more move from Henley in Arden to Alcester. It has been a great encouragement to have Canon John in Alcester as he was classically trained at Oxford and there is a first rate brain there for consultation when I need it. Then there was Julie and Andrew. We were really after them, as Julie in particular was a licensed reader and of a different background to me who clearly specialised in more informal types of worship. It did not take long before the deed was done and we signed her up at a special service. She soon got to work on the Family Service and thus brought hope and sustenance to those who found the Sung Eucharist as being not quite to their liking. She is a big girl with a big heart and she will always be a dear friend and colleague. Great fun at a party. I soon found out that she liked white wine and, that her husband was like me, a Real Ale fan! What more could I desire? But I must also mention Canon Hammer. Referred to by Caroline Newey as, "Toby Jug" he was probably one of the best theological brains in the country. He would occasionally help out and it was only when he had died that we found out much more about him. He had worked with his wife and with Tito's Partisans during the war to build railways in Yugoslavia. He would lecture theology to the Japanese in their own language and would pop up at big ecclesiastical events where he seemed to know everybody. His birthday was always recorded in the Times. When he was dying in hospital the consultants had to get in the top medical academics to explain to him what was going on. He wanted to know and they were not going to be able to sweep that under the carpet.

I started to get involved with local organisations and offered to go to France with the Twinning Group and preach in French at the Sunday service in Le Pallet. My offer was accepted with alacrity and so I needed to sort out my sermon and translate it into French. I decided to cheat and having produced a short sermon for the Feast of Pentecost, I toddled off to see Douglas Oldham, one of my regulars, who had been head of modern languages at Alcester Grammar School. He gave me a rather suspicious look as if to say, "I have dealt with boys like you before", but he did translate it for me! So off to France we went. I stayed with a vine grower (what bliss) and Henri could not have been more solicitous and on the Sunday he took me right into the vestry of the church of St. Vincent in Le Pallet. It was all typically very Gaelic and there was no sign of anything resembling organisation. Then a somewhat scruffy individual turned up with jeans and an open neck shirt. Yes! He was the priest, so we shook hands vigorously and I was taken into the church to get the feel of things. I had been asked about receiving communion, by all sorts of people so I thought that I had better sort this out quickly. I enquired and was asked a question as to whether I believed in the body and blood of Christ? Yes, I said. No problem said he, so I went outside and told the assembled Alcestrians that it was all OK. I well remember the queue that came. There were Baptists, Methodists, Anglicans, lapsed Romans and sitting in their places of honour were the mayors with their tricolour sashes. The French Roman Catholics are much more laid back and rather Low Church in some respects. I noticed that the priest took no notice of the Blessed Sacrament as we processed in, but needless to say, I genuflected and nobody seemed to bother about crossing themselves, so I felt that needed correction. I preached in both languages and then was invited to pray in French, so I prayed for the French President and then for the Queen. I heard afterwards that the French would never have dreamt of praying for their President, but had no problem at all in praying for the Queen of England. I was invited to stand at the altar and virtually concelebrated; it was great honour and a very memorable event. Needless to say, the whole visit was interspersed with stops for what was euphemistically referred to as, "Un petit degustation". The French were wonderful hosts and I would love to go back one day and preach again.

During this time of comparative frivolity other things of a more spiritual nature were happening beneath the surface. Now, I have always prayed for an increase in vocation to the ordained ministry and an increase in response to vocation and I cannot go any further without mentioning two colleagues. Both taught at Alcester Grammar School and both clearly had received, "the call". Would both they and the authorities recognise that call? Andy Shearn was a born Christian leader and it was only a matter of time before he retired as Headmaster and then offered himself at a selection conference and went to Queens College, from whence he was ordained in Coventry Cathedral. Andy now serves as a Non Stipendiary Minister at Studley and it was a great privilege to be asked to lay hands at his ordination to the priesthood. Then there was Richard Dobell who had been head of music and then transferred to be school bursar. We could all see that there was something going on there, but we had to get him off the organ stool and behind the altar, so to speak. Eventually he went to selection conference and was on his way to college. Now, I don't think that Alcester can take any credit for this fostering of vocation, but it was going on amongst us. Priests do not grow on trees, they have to be selected, trained properly and nurtured throughout their ministry and this all costs money. The foundation of the Christian Life must always be ministry and mission rather than maintenance.

It did not take very long before the Fire Brigade got to hear about my return to Warwickshire and as the chaplain who had been appointed by my father was about to retire, it was suggested that I might like to take his place? This I duly did with great ceremony and a full blown march up the High Street with massed bands and pipe band as well. I have to say, that it was all just a bit over the top. Even for me! Anyway, the one really good thing that came out of this was that I always went to the annual conference of fire brigade chaplains at Moreton in Marsh. Here I met up with all sorts of interesting people from right across the board. Even a minister from The Countess of Huntingdon's Connection. What about that! But we shared a common concern and although there was the inevitable Mickey taking, we all got on very well together. Moreton in Marsh is world famous in these matters. Just about every country in the world sends its fire fighters there at sometime for specialist training. There is a registered motorway, a high speed railway line, a merchant ship, a large hotel, a shopping mall, an oil drilling rig, a turbo prop plane and a helicopter crash. You name it, they have got it. The Madrid Fire Brigade drive there each year for training and the Dutch virtually live there on a permanent basis. There is now an earthquake shatter zone which was built quite deliberately to be superior to the one that the Americans had built. Then to cap it all, the Argentineans felt that it was a very long way for the South American Brigades to go for training, so they set up their own college. But they knew that nobody would use it unless it had been set up in conjunction with Moreton in Marsh and that the course had been properly moderated. This was done in due course, but everyone knows who is behind it all. It was a great joy to be elected as National Chairman for two years but more about the fire brigade later.

We started to have "Away Days" and even, "Away Weekends" I well remember playing a silent game of snooker with Nigel Boswell, Andrew Deeks and Andy Shearn at the Offchurch Retreat House. It was absolutely riotous and yet we were supposed to be on retreat. Then there was the weekend at the Bishop Mascall centre in Ludlow. Fortunately for me there was some free time on the Saturday afternoon which was just as well because that enabled me and Mike Dean to go to a pub and watch the final of the Rugby World Cup. It was the famous one when the Springboks won and Nelson Mandela uttered those immortal words to the Springbok Captain, "For years the springbok had been a symbol of oppression, but now it will be a symbol of hope". Then we went back to our duties and it was all part of a parish bonding process which eventually would bear much fruit. We also went to Hothorpe Hall near Market Harborough. Superb accommodation which had previously been owned by the English Lutherans, but now controlled by a private trust. Great opportunities for families to come together, for small group discussion and then an informal plenary session. We provided our own entertainment in the evening and although there was no bar, we were allowed to bring in our own refreshments. Sunday morning was great fun as Betty Gedge took a whole gang up to the village pub and treated them all to a round of drinks. I remember insisting that at least one meal should be in silence, but to prevent boredom, I would read something to them. I opted for the Village Cricket Match which ensured that the meal was far from being silent and I think I threw in for good measure a pen picture or two of Anglican Clergymen from the hand of no lesser a personage then Anthony Trollope. Then we had two trips to Courtfield on the Welsh Border which had been the home to the Vaughan family. We dined in style and were looked after by a Roman Catholic order known as the Millhill fathers. The priests were Irish and wonderful company, needless to say, there was a bar with prices at rock bottom and the boss man joined us on Saturday Night. He was great fun. It was here that I gained a greater appreciation of what the painting by Rembrandt of the Prodigal Son really meant. It has provided me with virtually limitless sermons and there was a copy of it hanging up to provide a backdrop for our deliberations. The Vaughan family were powerful Roman Catholics in their day and one of them went on to become the third cardinal Archbishop of Westminster. The family could trace their ancestry back there until at least the battle of Agincourt. All in all an amazing place with stupendous walks and the presence of peregrine falcons for those who like that sort of thing. It was some years later when I was walking the Wye valley walk that I looked up at Courtfield from the River Wye and perceived its almost mystical qualities from down in the valley. Again I would love to go back, but it has now been sold to the Vaughan family who wanted to move back into their ancestral home.

Cricket provided me with that glorious opportunity of combining a hobby with work. My sons have all played cricket for Alcester and Ragley Park Cricket Club and I became a member myself and played a few games and on a handful of occasions actually took up my favourite position behind the stumps as wicket keeper. Then I had a chat after a confirmation service with the Chaplain of Warwick University who had brought along a couple of candidates. Clive Gregory was the Captain of the Diocesan Clergy Cricket team; he now plays for Lichfield and is also Bishop of Wolverhampton into the bargain. Clive told me about the delights of the Church Times Cricket Competition which is the longest established restricted overs competition in the country. I was hooked and I soon took over as secretary as I was able to arrange for Ragley Park to be made available, which went down very well indeed. There are so many stories to tell, but the most important factor was that clergy of all sorts and shades of opinion could get together. Many a diocesan officer has confessed that such gatherings had proved to be very fruitful. I got to know clergy who came from the opposite end of the candle to me and can now count many an evangelical priest as a friend.

On one famous occasion we advanced to the quarter final with a match against Exeter which I fixed on the grounds of Wells Cathedral School. I drove down and spent most of the journey discussing Celtic spirituality with Paul Hunt and leaving Steve Tash in the back seat to silently scan the pages of the Guardian. I had said that I wanted to call at my favourite cider farm and fill up with the fermented juice of the apple. We arrived at Lands End Farm, Mudgeley, not far from Wedmore. It was an education for my colleagues as the barn looked like a public urinal and there were these old boys just sitting on milking pails and dispensing cider into small plastic containers! We carried on to Wells and I set up shop with my score sheet and my cider. It was an historic win and we all met up in the Fountain Inn, of blessed memory afterwards for an evening meal. But danger lurked on the horizon, because we had been drawn against Oxford for our semi final match. I arranged for the match to be played at Moreton in Marsh, which had occasional county matches played there, so it seemed eminently suitable. We received apostolic blessings from our president, Bishop Anthony and there was a prayer meeting before we took to the field. It was disastrous. We were bowled out for 19 runs. Richard Deimel and I put on 10 runs for the last wicket. The least said about that game the better!

There was a game that I fixed at Ragley for Lichfield to play Oxford. All was proceeding apace and the sheep were baa-ing in their soft pastures, when one of the Lichfield batsmen drove the ball towards the boundary. We could all see that the ball had crossed over the boundary rope, but the Oxford fielder just picked up the ball and threw it back to the keeper without signalling a boundary. The skipper of Lichfield was already padded up. He was a Prebendary of the Cathedral and decided to let his views be known. Up he jumped and at the top of his voice shouted out,

"You lying S—". He was incandescent with fury. Dick Allen from Bath and Wells and Phil Searle from Lichfield were great characters, they both had a deep love for souls, they were both fast bowlers with very long hair and they both enjoyed copious draughts of ale. Then there was the time when we could not find the ground where Gloucester was waiting to play us. We ended up in a farmyard and arrived quite late, to find a ground in the middle of nowhere with no electricity and only a feeble supply of water. We won that match and adjourned to an ancient pub just down the road. It was then that Steve Burch asked if I would be prepared to give him a reference as he had been asked to apply for the vacant living of St. James Fletchampstead in Coventry. Little did I know at that time how that move would affect me some years later!

I decided to become even more involved with clergy cricket and took on the mantle of acting as secretary of the midlands group. Each year we have a meeting in Alcester at the Holly Bush where I lay on lunch and a few beers. We have a chat and then sort out the fixtures, ensuring that some inconsiderate Bishop has not fixed a diocesan conference for a Monday in either May or June. One year this was a big problem and so the following year the editor of the Church Times did write to the Bishops and ask for their "kind consideration". In Coventry diocese we now have the problem of arranging a team. The rules have been changed and in some cases bent. At the end of the day, we just want a game and a chance to meet up. Licensed readers may now play and so can those who hold a bishop's licence. That is open to interpretation and I have used that flexibility for my big son Mark to play and also for Andrew Deeks to turn his hand. We still meet up and just occasionally we are treated to a game against Worcester on the county ground itself where we are greeted by the Chief Executive who arranges for a courtesy tea. Why? Do I hear you ask? Well it is quite simple really because the cathedral owns the land. Every now and again, the Dean can be seen in high-class reserved seating. Barchester still rules! I no longer play, but I arrange the games, fix the grounds not just for us, but for other teams who need a neutral venue and do the scoring. When we play at Ragley, I also run the bar and what is good to know is that the estate wrote into the new lease that arrangements could always be made for the clergy of the Established Church to play cricket.

Ragley is in Arrow parish and there are still stories around to this day which refer to parishioners sitting on a bench to watch a game and then walking back to church for evensong when the bell tolled. Arrow is a delightful church and has had some delightful characters. One of whom was the organist in my time, namely, Alan Hunt. Alan was the very last Headmaster of Bidford High School and was probably the most under rated organist in South Warwickshire. He played to a high standard and could boast that his organ teacher had been taught by Elgar. Alan used to slide off his stool during my sermon and before I realised what was going on he had come round the front and was beginning to debate with me. He liked to play all the verses for a hymn and if I decided to limit the number of verses, there would be a long and loud groan from the direction of the organ. He could also compose and would do so under some form of pseudonym to fool us all. His death was a great loss to the Arrow community as was the death of that evergreen personality, Harry Hayton who had flown in Lancaster Bombers in the war and gone on to achieve high rank in the police force. Harry loved to talk and also to organise quizzes at the village hall. They were memorable occasions, coupled with much laughter. We shall miss both those faithful parishioners in the years to come. Like their fellow worshippers, they could see the condition of the church was deteriorating and that although it would be possible to cut and paste, so to speak, the long term prognosis was not good. Money speaks in these cases and what with the quota payments which are a requisite first charge on the parish finances, plus the horrendous costs of repair to ancient churches, then the future is very bleak indeed. Slowly but surely, Arrow and other churches are reluctantly moving to the view that worship and ministry are going to have to be much more centralised. How we do this and sensitively deal with the flesh and blood which makes up even a small congregation, remains to be seen.

Chapter 14

ROTARY CLUB OF ALCESTER ST. NICHOLAS

Rotary became a big part of my life as I was visited and told that the members of this evening club would like me to join. In those days, the club met up at the Moat House but members were becoming increasingly fed up with the arrangements there and expressed their frustration. On one particular occasion we had been waiting for some time and no food came, so the President, who was a most impressive black American, spoke in very loud tones that we were waiting. He did this about half a dozen times with increased volume at each repeat. Eventually the food came and it was an insult just consisting of about one cubic inch of fish and a hint of vegetable. That did it and we transferred to the Swan in the middle of the town which was better for me as I had a eucharist on Tuesday nights and could then walk down after the service. I enjoyed my time with this very small club which had been a breakaway from the mother club of Alcester some twenty years previously. They preferred to meet for lunch and remain totally male, whereas we liked the idea of an evening meeting without the need to rush back to work after lunch, and, we had no problem with female company. So there were many happy times at the Swan and I soon became speaker secretary which, as the title implies meant that I could use my various contacts to obtain the services of visiting speakers. On one occasion we had a musical evening with Mick Perrier and he got us to compose music on the hoof, we had visits from RSPB, Nature Trusts, the Fire Brigade, and Politicians etc. There were also the inevitable visits, to breweries and also a visit to a dog track where I subscribed to the wisdom of my grandfather who always reckoned that he would put money on the second favourite. He would have a good night out, he would never make much money neither would he lose much money. It worked!

We supported the local high blood pressure campaign and arranged to take some of the old folk to the theatre in Redditch. We were rapidly becoming a *very old club*, but there were still events that could be organised without too much effort. I decided to arrange some fishing matches for the youngsters down on the river by the Stratford Road. I was very grateful to Neil Johnson for kind permission to access his waters. In fact it was a most satisfactory arrangement because this led to the local angling club being able to access their own waters by a much easier route and also for them to be able to fish on what had been their old waters of some years ago. All in all, a most satisfactory arrangement and Rotary was seen to be instrumental in setting this up. We had many a happy time there, the parents came, the scouts set up a gazebo and hot drinks were served. The local angling fraternity joined up to give advice and the manufacturers were leant on to provide lots of prizes.

But it was clear to me that our days were numbered and that after a few departures, due, for the most part, to there being a personality issue we were down to ten members. Now, I know for a fact that you really cannot run a club on that number of members. My late father had been President of Royal Leamington Spa Club, so I knew the form. Then there was the compelling logic of our Secretary, John Cooper (known as J.C.) who, with a recent masters degree in English from Warwick University was not going to let us get away with lots of dithering. So we decided we would carry on for one more year. Guess who would be the new President? Perhaps the thinking of the members was that if there was going to be the need for last rites then who better than a priestly President to officiate at such a ceremony? My own view was that we would go out with a bang and hold our heads up. This we did in some style by taking the lead in instigating the Boy Bishop Procession up the High Street on December 6th the Feast of St. Nicholas. It did not take long to arrange for a road closure order, for charities to book space for a street stall and for me to arrange a firework display, plus roasting of the pig and special beers to be brewed. It went a bomb. I admit to taking a chance, but I was able to buy in some favours and we had a great procession led by a thurifer, swinging the incense pot, the band, morris dancers who had to be dragged out of the pub, Fire personnel, the choir and anyone who felt like joining in with the Boy Bishop and his attendants seated in a chariot kindly provided by the local Round Table. I took up the rear, wearing a biretta, much to my wife's disgust, and, escorted by my wardens, liberally sprinkled the crowds with Holy water. The whole event exceeded my wildest expectations and there must have been close on 2000 persons in the High Street that night. St. Nicholas Night has now become a firm favourite in the local calendar and is always held on December 6th. We have added various other attractions such as the Boy Bishop switching on the light on the tree accompanied by the High Bailiff who switches on the crown which tops out the tower. We now finish with that delightful service of Compline by candlelight and sung to Gregorian chant. Our mission statement is to provide an evening out for the community and to make some modest payments to youth related activities if we have a surplus.

But I still had the annual conference to go to in Manchester, which I had really been looking forward to. Free transport on the tram network was a great attraction for me, so I stayed with some former members of my youth club, now well into their fifties out at Hale which meant that there was fairly easy access to the trams at Altrincham. I met some first rate people at Conference, including the National President who was a most impressive person. We were introduced and so the traditional greeting is just, "Mr. President" whether it was the National President or the President of the smallest club. I was suitably gratified and explained that we had taken the decision to call it a day. He was most sympathetic and when I told him that I did not believe in a slow and painful death, but rather, a good death, a decent burial and a glorious resurrection, he asked if he could quote me at some point in the future. I did manage to view some of the famous Lowry paintings and to take out my friends for a slap up meal which my club said they would pay for and then it was home for Mark's birthday.

There is one other project that we entered into and that was a bucket shake for the victims of the Tsunami Disaster in the Indian Ocean down at Hopkins Precinct. Everyone was extremely generous and we were able to support the Mother Club who had thought of the idea in the first place. Then I went home to find that Hilary was on the phone and that something serious had happened. My mother had died and I spoke to the home where she had been living in Leamington Spa and told them not to worry as they were so apologetic as if it were their fault. Mum had died very peacefully sitting in her chair and having just had a cup of coffee. It was what she would have wanted. But I did not have time to grieve because there was a funeral to take at the Redditch Crematorium and I was running late already. Fortunately I arrived in time without giving anything away and after the service, said to Ted the Dead (undertaker), "I have some business for you!" The next day, I bumped into a parishioner who told me that I was now an orphan. I had not thought of it as being like that. But at the end of the day you just have to get on with it. The business of parish life carries you on and as I did know one or two tricks of the trade, so to speak, I was able to cut a few corners before the funeral service which was to be held at Lillington where I had found my vocation all those years ago. I asked if I might celebrate a requiem mass and then the priest invited me to give the address from the pulpit at the service the next day. It was all very low key, but also very simple and very dignified. I did have a slight twinge of guilt in that I did not get over to see her on Christmas day, but we all went over as a family on Boxing Day and Mark, who she was very fond of, had called to see her the day before she died. It is at times like this that you are eternally grateful for the training that you received. There is a hidden part to all this and it kicks in as long as you let it. I did not have too much difficulty in coping over the months; despite still grieving for my father from all those years ago. It made me think again about the way I do funerals and my general approach to the initial visit and the subsequent follow up. But there was still one more office of the church that I needed to perform for my mother and that was to go down to Minehead and inter her ashes alongside those of my father in the grave of his parents. This meant taking a few days off, but we managed it and parked for a while outside the house that she had lived in as a girl back in the 1930s.The cemetery lies just out of town and only a few yards from the boundary of the National Park of Exmoor. And so, there, with the North Hill looking down on us I laid her mortal remains to rest close to the graves of her brothers who had died all those years ago and close to the graves of my great grandparents. I have since found out that parishioners of mine have the grave of one of their sets of parents also in Minehead cemetery. We have an arrangement, whereby if we are in town, then we always put flowers on their family grave and they always reciprocate.

Needless to say, there was the inevitable sorting out of the estate and the eventual swearing of probate. It was all very straightforward as the house came to me and I then put it into both our names. Then came the inevitable final bill. It seemed quite hefty and I have never known the legal profession to be other than very professional, for which, of course you pay. But I contented myself with the fact that I had recently wound up the estate of an aunt over in Norfolk and she had, in my opinion, foolishly appointed one of the clearing banks to do the job. I could not believe how greedy they were and they simply siphoned off very substantial sums of money at ever increasing intervals.

So the final days of our Rotary club approached and we decided to invite as many former members as we could track down to our last meeting when it had been decided that after the final toast of, "Rotary and Peace the World over", I would then take off my chain, kiss the medallion and then lay it on the table. Gwen Brinson who was Vice President would do the same. The day came and there were about 25 past and present members sitting down for the last rites. It was all very enjoyable and we went out on a positive note with the agreement that we would continue to meet once each month for dinner and attempt to carry on with the community projects that had exercised our minds when we were in Rotary. We still meet seven years later and the numbers remain the same, with one unexpected addition and the occasional visitor. So perhaps in some ways, nothing has changed, but that is what the problem has been with Alcester and perhaps in the not too distant future, this re-organised group will need a good death, a decent burial and a glorious resurrection. It is not for me to say but, like other groups in the town, we need to remember the dictum of Blessed John Henry, Cardinal Newman, that to change is to grow and to change often is to move towards perfection. Is that asking too much?

Chapter 15

THE CREATION OF THE ALCESTER MINSTER CHURCHES

For some years I had seen the writing on the wall as far as the large number of independent parish churches was concerned. The political process throughout the country meant the merging of previously separate entities and in some cases the actual removal of same from very existence. The church could not expect to be immune from such changes in society and, in any case the number of people who were gracing the doors of the churches with their presence had fallen dramatically. As I write this book, there are now moves afoot to merge dioceses, and I for one, heartily support such an initiative. I had come to Alcester to take on one of the early, "mergers" which added Arrow with Weethley to Alcester. I had cast my eyes around and formulated some ideas as to how this might further pan out. However, the Church of England tended to wait until something happened before actually doing anything. The cut and paste method had served it well in the past and, in any case parishioners did not like change. We had all been reactive rather than proactive. My big bug bear, Synodical Government had also delayed the process and it was only when David Hall the Rural Dean gave me a call and said that he had an idea that he would like to discuss with me, that I realised that something was actually on the boiler.

Father David Hall recalled that I had spoken at Clergy Chapter of my enthusiasm for a book, entitled, "Parochial Vision" which had talked about going backwards so as to go forward. I must confess that it appealed to me with my somewhat traditional background. The idea was to re-create a grouping that had served the church well in the past, when a church in a large village or small town had sent out priests to celebrate mass and to preach in the small villages and hamlets round about. This was at the time when there were not very many church buildings, but now of course that was not the case and there had to be changes in staffing levels. Priests have to be trained and paid, as I have said before in this book. With the broad sweep of its establishment remit, the Church of England did not have enough priests even with the cover provided by non stipendiary clergy to ensure that every church had its own "vicar". This seemed to be a new way forward and a refreshing change from Team Ministries which had not always endeared themselves to those who sit in the pews. There would be a lot of training so that the laity could take on both liturgical and pastoral duties and so many of the services would be of a non sacramental nature. Alcester was in the happy position of having a handful of retired clergy who were happy to take some services and what with a goodly gathering of licensed readers, there were distinct possibilities. Alcester St. Nicholas would be expected to take initiatives, to provide resources and to be a focus for mission across the area. Would I be interested? The answer was, yes. Suddenly the Church of England clicked into action and in an amazingly short time, the deal was done and I was to take on responsibility for five additional churches (inclusive of three PCCs). A friend of mine told me in very blunt language that I was a b—— fool! However, I was all for it, especially as there were to be some glorious churches on the patch. So, after a fright when it appeared that one side of the diocese was talking about one particular manifestation and another part had completely different ideas, it was agreed that we should meet. Representatives were gathered together and we met for an inaugural meeting at Sambourne Church when it was agreed that the Minster grouping should be created with a licensing by Bishop John of Warwick in about six months time. I remember the meeting well, because John Parr from Haselor, very kindly invited us all to have a drink at the Green Dragon and the beer was absolutely lousy! I have not been in there since, but John and I still have a laugh about it. But perhaps now I ought to tell you something about the churches which are all very different.

I enjoy walking and on a couple of times, some of us have endeavoured to both create and walk, "The Minster Way", starting at Sambourne. This church has no dedication and has not been consecrated. At first sight it does not look very appealing, but you would be very wrong in writing it off. It is a dual purpose building and with minimum amounts of labour, the altar can be curtained off, leaving the rest of the building for community use. There are good kitchen and toilet facilities and, as I have told the parishioners there, they do not have to spend vast amounts of time on faculty applications, because the ecclesiastical measure does not apply in unconsecrated buildings. To my mind, that is a big advantage. Linked to Sambourne is the historically important church of St. Peter in Coughton. It is next door to the National Trust property of Coughton Court with all its Gunpowder Plot connotations. There are some superb stained glass windows in place and some ancient tombstones relating to the Throckmorton family. It is always a great joy to celebrate there and feel the medieval atmosphere oozing out! Relationships with the National Trust are excellent. The next stop on the Minster Way is the Church of St. Mary Magdalen in Great Alne. This is set back from the main road and looks out onto meadow land. It is a lovely little church, and does have the advantage of a balcony for extra seating. There is a school, as there is at Coughton and there is also a reasonably sized pub with restaurant, in addition there is a first rate village memorial hall with excellent facilities. Great Alne is linked to Kinwarton with its church of St. Mary the Virgin being a Grade 1 listed building set out by the fields and away from the main centre of population. There is a National Trust dovecote next door. The church has been lovingly cared for and is ideal for healing services and for the sacrament of penance. Again, I have a wonderful feeling of continuity whenever I celebrate there. Both Kinwarton and Great Alne share a PCC. Last but not least, there is the church of St. Mary and All Saints situated on a hill between the village of Haselor and the hamlet of Walcote. You need to climb to get up there, but the view is good and on one particular Christmas when I went up there for the morning service and the whole countryside was covered in thick snow, I experienced what can only be termed a beautiful, freezing incandescence. Memorable indeed was that morning and you could even see the print of the tail of the fox in the snow!

So we started up together with Alcester, Arrow and Weethley. I took the view from those early days that it would take some time to bed down, possibly a generation or two. And there was also the possibility of changes to its shape in the future. I have been proved correct in this respect, I just wish some of this could have been sorted out at an earlier date. However, we did have another Founding Father, so to speak, in the figure of an ear-ringed priest called Father Roger Morris. He is now an Archdeacon, but was very good to me and I was always pleased to see him because he just happened to be an aficionado of Real Ale. On at least three occasions the two of us arranged a Pints of View session in the pubs of Alcester, I think it is time that I arranged another one! Roger got us thinking about our missionary priorities and advised us always to play to our strengths. He very willingly attended two of our day conferences where he took the lead.

Then of course we needed to sort out services and cover for those services. Needless to say, we could not always provide for all requests. To my mind it was important that each church should have one celebration of the Holy Eucharist per month with some extra services conducted by clergy and readers. Basically, the bigger the church or the greater the number of worshippers, then the greater the number of services. Where there were gaps, then we suggested that the laity might like to officiate occasionally, having undergone suitable training which my colleagues were very eager to provide. This has worked to a degree, but occasionally we cannot manage and I have to say that at least there is a guarantee of regular services at Alcester. I am very indebted to John Berry, who is now employed as Administrator, because he takes on the thankless job of arranging the services and trying to keep everyone happy. It is hoped that in the not too distant future, Alcester will be able to provide fully equipped office accommodation which will help to centralise administration and improve communication between the eight churches.

We have had our successes, just as we have had our failures. The coming together for special services such as the Advent Carol service which does the rounds and likewise the monthly Minster Praise service has been well received. On the fifth Sunday, the villages meet together to worship with a Eucharist and with one exception I have just about managed to keep the first Sunday free so that there is just one main service at Alcester. There needs to be at least an attempt at demonstrating to the wider world that there is a sense of some sort of unity. Now, I am not so naïve as to think that everyone from the villages will be rushing to come to Alcester, even if they come to Alcester for their daily requirements, but at least it gives my colleagues a Sunday off and that applies to some over worked wardens in the villages as well.

The chief benefit for me was the inheritance, so to speak, of a team of licensed readers which brought our number up to six, with Gill from Arrow, having recently been licensed. So there was Julie, Daphne, Gill, John, Pat and Ted. I could not have asked for more loyal colleagues and they brought into the equation their own very special gifts and best of all a different expression of churchmanship. I think that we have all benefited from this, and I certainly have. However we felt that we deserved the additional services of a priest. We had been well served by other retired priests in the minster area. I have already mentioned Canon John Cooke, but there was also Father John Cook who had been a U.S.P.G. missionary out in Singapore with his wife Daphne, the reader. Then there was Padre Jim Symonds who had served in the army, plus Dr. Michael Watson and Canon Alan Boddington, for whom I am very grateful for helping out from time to time; but at the end of the day, it would be very wrong to rely totally on them as they are all retired. Then there was the great joy with the wish of Dr. Julian Davey to want to come and minister with us which meant that we could begin to draw up some areas of pastoral responsibility. One more House for Duty priest would do the trick, especially if we wanted to set up a training programme.

It was then that with the appropriate permissions granted, we advertised in the Church Times. There was only one applicant, but he had been sent by God and of that, we all had no doubt. Mike and Charmian came to be with us from May 2010. Mike is a former Sergeant Major in the Army who came from the opposite end of the liturgical candle to me. He is as low Church as I am high church, which means that we get on well. When I looked at the application I was particularly interested in the identity of his Team Rector and main referee, namely Canon David Taylor in Congleton. A quick check in Crockford's Clerical Directory and it proved to be a former colleague of mine who had been a licensed reader in Newton Aycliffe. What a stroke of luck, because I had a very high opinion of David and so a telephone call soon ensued. I was told that with Mike, what you saw was what you got. Totally dependable, and so he was and continues to be to this day. It was good to meet up with David again at the licensing service for Mike and talk about our times in the Kingdom of Northumbria.

So we were up to full compliment and could begin to plan ahead and as I believe in giving as much notice as possible, I told my colleagues that I intended to retire by the end of 2012. I also did not want them to hang around indefinitely during an interregnum, as had happened in the past.

Chapter 16

THE YEAR 2007, SOME JOY, BUT A LOT OF SORROW

By this time there had been changes with respect towards Alcester. Chris and Marion had taken over from Doug and Gill and brought with them, their own distinctive gifts. Doug had been Lay Chair of the Deanery Synod, whereas Gill was the driving force behind the pastoral initiatives with special reference to funeral follow up. Yet again, I was to be very fortunate with my new colleagues.

My dear friend and colleague Richard Dobell had been with me for a few years having transferred over from St. James Alveston, where he had been since ordination. Richard had a very distinctive style in preaching and was dearly loved by all who met him. There was great joy when he married Jan and a very large gathering of the teaching profession turned up to support them on their big day. It was some time later when Richard was conducting a baptism service, that afterwards some medics who had been present suggested that he needed to see a doctor. There was a growth close to the brain which appeared to be benign, but it was suggested that an operation to remove it was necessary. This was booked in for after Easter and so on the feast of the Resurrection, Richard preached and celebrated at Weethley and then came up to St. Nicholas to celebrate here, with me preaching. He was not to celebrate again as after the operation a few days later, complications set in and I received an urgent phone call to go over to the Walsgrave Hospital in Coventry to administer the last rites and to take my farewell of my friend. I was glad that Hilary could come with me on that occasion as hospitals are not my favourite sort of building. Jan and her daughters were there and Andy Shearn appeared which gave me the opportunity to ask him if he would give the address at the forthcoming funeral. We spent some time with the family and then it was opportune to leave them together for those last very precious minutes. The subsequent funeral was massive and I needed to arrange for traffic to be re-directed in the town, such was the popularity of Richard! I have to say that the walk to the grave was especially difficult, but on the other hand it would have been far worse for Jan.

It is on these occasions that delayed shocks sets in and I had actually been booked in to take a wedding on the same day, in fact a former pupil of Richard. Julian Davey moved in decisively and told me that there was no way I would be able to go from such a tragedy to a joyful occasion. He was quite right. He also knew that fairly recently I had been dealing with the burial of a new born baby that had been found in the river, which attracted national attention, so I was feeling tender in that respect. But as always, the Lord brings something new and positive out of these occasions and this was particularly relevant to our family. Mark had married Helen in St. Nicholas Church a few years previously and the Officiant had been Richard! It appears that Richard had been talking to Mark and had suggested that he might have a calling to the ordained ministry. Now we had not seen it, but Richard had, with the result that this coming June, Mark will be ordained deacon in Norwich Cathedral. A great day for Mark, Helen and our two grandsons, Joel and Nathan. Also, of course, some very happy memories of Richard. What is more, even when she was in the middle of her grief, Jan insisted that Hilary and I go away together to celebrate our 30th wedding anniversary. This we did at Dunster, close to Minehead and so we were able to tidy up the family graves and walk up on Exmoor.

On return, it was back to normality as far as that is ever possible in parish life, but not for long. I forget the actual date, but in July it started to rain one day and it rained and it rained well into the next day. Before we knew it, we were in for big time flooding. Much work had been done on the south side of the town since the last flood in 1999 and there was no ingress of water from that direction, but it penetrated on the north side of the town and swung around the west side to appear on the south side and come up the High Street. The pubs down that end of town began to close down and the regulars started to move out and further up. This process carried on for a while until they reached the Three Tuns, which with its stone flag floor and basic furniture was able to offer a haven to the drinkers. On our side, the waters swept along Moorfield Road which had previously been the site of the river course many years previously and started to surround the newly constructed Guide and Scout Headquarters.

We went down to see what we could do to help and had only just left our house when we saw this dark blob coming up our drive. It was therefore wellies and they were only just high enough for us to get to the Headquarters without getting wet. After some desultory efforts to remove certain contents and put them in a safe place, it was obvious to me that we were wasting our time and I actually said that this was now an insurance job, and let's get the hell out of it and wait for the floodwater to disperse. We trudged home and began to hear of the horror stories that surrounded us. All in all, about 150 properties were affected by flood water, rather more than Stratford which got all the publicity for just a few buildings. After some clearing up the next day, I summoned a meeting of the Great and the Good of Alcester and asked for money! I remembered after the 1999 flood, that some relief had been given to the very badly stricken families and this seemed to be the opportunity to do it again.

The meeting was good humoured but with serious intent. I knew that some of the charities with which I was associated had ample funds, so I got to work and arranged for meetings to be held at short notice which would authorise payments into a common flood fund. We eventually arranged for close on £5,000 to be gathered in and decided to make a proper list of affected homes and then to send out printed compliment slips from the community together with cash to the sum of £25. The message said that the recipient should use the money as they thought fit: paying towards increased heating bills, the cost of a meal out, or a take away in! Whatever they wanted. When I went about on my rounds with the envelopes, you could easily be mistaken into thinking that you had given them a bar of solid gold, rather than £25. Their thanks were profuse and very gratifying, the community was pulling together and most of the water by this time had subsided and all that was left was mud. With there having been two big floods with considerable damage within the space of eight years, questions were beginning to be asked and Insurance Companies were darkly muttering about restricting cover in the future. I am sure we are very grateful for the efforts of our elected councillors in insisting that something had to be done and substantial work has now been executed which will lessen the future risk considerably. What else was there to come?

Holiday time came and went and we all returned to school, so to speak. It was a Saturday morning, I remember it well. It was the festival of the Holy Cross and as it was a Saturday morning we treated ourselves to a mug of tea in bed. For once the post had come rather early and there was a letter from Bishop Colin, so I opened it and blinked. I read it once more and blinked again. I was to be appointed an Honorary Canon of Coventry Cathedral. I sprinted upstairs to impart the good news and then wondered why. Various thoughts came into my mind, but it appears that the main reason was that I had been very willingly to pick up the concept of the Minster Churches. I must confess that I had thought some time back that I had "missed the boat". Clergy are no different to anyone else, so I had put it behind me and got on with being a full time parish priest. The surprise was even more delightful and it was a wonderful letter from Bishop Colin, who had also appointed a second Anglo Catholic Priest, Father Kit from St. Luke's Holbrooks. Did I accept? Yes I did. What now?

The date for the collation and installation had been fixed for November 3rd which was no problem for me at that time. This seemed to be a good opportunity to have a party, and as the Town Hall had already been booked it was suggested that I use the Fire Station, which was a great idea because my father had built the station when he had been Chief and he had added a licensed bar so that the station could relate to the local community. Then I needed to order the ecclesiastical gear which put me back rather more than I had thought. For the first time I would be wearing preaching bands, known as walrus whiskers in the trade and a different colour cassock somewhat akin to mushroom colour and known as, "Crush Mush" I needed a new black cassock as well, so I ordered a soutane with the red trimming. The day approached rapidly and the parish got together two coach loads of supporters, so I was really looking forward to it. Then we came to the day before, November 2nd the Festival of All Souls. I had a wedding in the afternoon and met up with some old friends from Claverdon RFC who I had played against many years ago. The enjoyment of the wedding and meeting up with old friends began to disappear as I prepared to celebrate Requiem Mass at 7.00pm. I returned home having heard on the news that there was a big fire at Atherstone on Stour. I didn't think much of it until at about 8.00pm I had a phone call from the police to say that four fire-fighters had gone into the fire wearing breathing apparatus and had not come out. It was suggested that I get down to the station, where I was to remain until about 5.00am the next morning. I have never experienced anything like it before and do not want to repeat it. Families were coming in, they were asking questions. How? What? Why? I spent most of my time serving up hot drinks, occasionally serving drinks from the bar and generally making myself useful. It was not the time to start bible bashing or offering explanations. I am so glad that I was just there. As the night proceeded, I began to unwind in my mind what might actually happen now as there were two Alcester lads amongst the missing. I could envisage the press and the television. I was likely to be involved anyway as until two weeks previously I had been the National Chair of the Fire-fighters Chaplains and in any case I had done media training; this was going to be big time. I was also known for occasionally speaking out on some issues. They would be waiting and sure enough they were. We decided at 5.00am that there was no point in staying at the station and that we would meet up again by 10.00am so I went home to be guided up Old Rectory Garden by a comet which was above. It was almost like Bethlehem.

I had just about enough time to snatch a couple of hours sleep and then phone Sally Staley the Head of St. Nicholas School and ask if I might transfer my party from the Fire Station to the School as there was no way that it could take place at Station 37. With that sorted, I made it back down to the station to find even bigger crowds and a growing realisation that nobody was going to be brought out alive from the blaze. It was at this time that I had to ask if someone could help in removing the drinks for the party. Thank goodness, it was all sorted in next to no time as some of the retained fire-fighters drew off all the beer from the cask into plastic containers and we delivered it all to the school. I then had to get home and prepare myself for the licensing, by which time there had already been a call from Bishop Colin who had been told of the events at Diocesan Synod.

Would I be in the Cathedral? Most certainly and I had to get a move on and arrive for the rehearsal. After a while we took a break and I was then told that the press were looking for me at the back of the cathedral. Still, I was lucky because it was my old friend Keith from Coventry and Warwickshire Radio and with another reporter, I answered questions until the time came for the service. Bishop Colin told the congregation a little about the history of the new candidates and needless to say, he alluded heavily to the events of the night before. Then we were led to our stalls in the Choir. I must confess that I reckon I have the best seat in the House. I am immediately behind the Diocesan Bishop, so I can keep an eye on him. I have a superb view of the organ consol with its four manuals and last but not least I am at the end of the row, so if the sermon goes on and I need a comfort break, then nothing could be easier. At the end of the service, there was a chance to meet up with my parishioners and friends and then stay around for photographs with Hilary, Mark and Helen, Peter and Stephen. Then it was back to Alcester for the party and what was also to come with the press, because the next morning I was on national breakfast television and within a few days had been interviewed on all channels. Channel 5 walked up my drive and asked for an interview. As it was convenient for me, I said that I could do an interview at that instant, so they went back very contented. I forget how many times I went back to the station. The families were almost living there and on occasions some of the local catering establishments delivered hot food gratis. I was grateful to Bishop Colin for allowing me to become in reality a full time Chaplain for as long as it took. There were countless meetings, some ceremonies as well as trips to the scene of the disaster where I saw appliances from throughout the country.

There is a long story to be told about November 2nd 2007 and it needs someone else to write it down. Ultimately this will have to be done and so my remarks here are fairly low key with just a few stories. Eventually the bodies were recovered and arrangements made for the funerals. I took the funerals of Ashley and Darren at Alcester and both brought massive turn outs. We then needed to plan for a big service in the cathedral for some time in January. But after a few weeks I noticed just a little change at Station 37. I was down there yet again and whilst up in the lounge, I noticed that one of the local fire-fighters had brought his car in for a car wash. That may not seem to be earth shattering, but I knew enough about the retained guys to know that this meant the start of the beginning to getting back to normal. There was then the return of their appliance for which they had longed. The Chief offered them a new state of the arts appliance, but no, they wanted their old appliance back and I was very grateful to Bishop John of Warwick for turning out that night as it was greeted with due solemnity and virtually a full blown parade.

It was good to serve with my father's old brigade. There were still a few around who remembered him and then there were new colleagues to get to know. Soon we had to really start planning for the big service to which every Fire Chief was to be invited and representatives from every brigade. I was over the moon when I found out that most of my former colleagues from the chaplaincy had decided to come and add their support. In the end there were forty five chaplains there of every shape and liturgical size. Chaplains came from Northumbria and Scotland as well as Ulster. It was a very moving service and I had asked that I might preach and it will probably be the only time when I will ever preach to a congregation of over 2,000. It all went well although I have to admit to being a little worried about the length of the cathedral cope which was draped over my shoulders; the last thing I wanted to do was to trip up while ascending the steps to the pulpit. I had done that many years previously when preaching at evensong with a large contingent of Harbury RFC present and was not going to repeat it!

So how do I finish off this chapter? All I can say is that year left an indelible mark on my soul, on my very being. I am grateful to Hilary and the family for their support, also to Jan and to the Warwickshire Fire Brigade. You cannot teach an old dog new tricks, and it will always be the Brigade as far as I am concerned. And I sincerely hope that there will always be a place for the Retained Crews. They are the life blood of local communities and like the Territorial Army, they fight alongside the full timers and you cannot tell the difference!

EPILOGUE

I have written this book in a bit of a hurry, somewhat like my great hero, Blessed John Henry, Cardinal Newman when he wrote the "Apologia". There is only one year left before I retire from full time ministry and for this last year I need to be doing other things. Therefore I know that some stories have been left out, partly for the reasons mentioned, but also because sensitivity and priestly confidentiality prohibit such inclusion! So to conclude with what must be the longest epistle that I have ever written, let alone preached, I am going to return to the basics of a priest's pastoral life, which are encompassed in "hatching, matching and dispatching" plus a few incidental stories including my life as a union rep, before finally signing off.

I may be a bit old fashioned, but I believe that at baptism something actually happens and that God acts. He acts, irrespective of the faith or lack of faith of the parents and godparents. I have always called into question the need in some churches to erect an obstacle course to satisfy a particular theological position and yet I have to admit that my patience has been sorely tried on more than one occasion. It was not long ago when my friend Chris Baker told me that he had been driving up Alcester High Street one Sunday when suddenly all the pub front doors opened, the pubs emptied and the drinkers made their way up to church for what clearly was going to be a baptism. It was quite an occasion and I have to admit that I all but lost my cool. With the creation of the Ministry Leadership Team, I was able to discuss this matter with my colleagues and to spin off ideas which I found very useful. It all seemed to be taken so much for granted and I felt that I was beginning to compromise my integrity. So what we do now is to invite parents to attend the showing of a DVD from the Church Pastoral Aid Society which sets out in an understandable form the basic requirements. This has proved to be very helpful to all concerned and so at least there is not so much, "take what you want and when you want attitude". I remember my very first baptism, the baby was called Esther Louise and I was delighted when she looked me up many years later so that I was able to baptise her own baby! I have never dropped the baby and nothing really horrendous has ever happened. On two occasions there had been a leak and when I went to gather up water for the actual baptism I had to scrape up a few drops from where I could find them. Having said that, it has been, and always will be a privilege to administer this sacrament, especially in respect of Mark, Peter and Stephen.

It is an equal privilege to celebrate a wedding. I well remember my first and I was actually challenged by the bride as to how many weddings I had taken before. I was able to say in all truthfulness that it was the first time for all of us, in my case the numbers would increase, but in their case it would remain one. I am pleased to say that is the case today because the couple have kept in touch. There was the added bonus that the bride's mother-in-law started coming to church and was eventually confirmed. When I moved to Shottery, I inherited a double booking! Fortunately for me, both couples thought it was a huge joke and we sorted the problem by each couple agreeing to go forward/go back a half hour, and also to arrive on time with one party coming out of church one way and the next party arriving by another way. A few months afterwards I took a wedding that was almost a copy of a mafia gathering. Everyone was well kitted out, hardly anything was said and everyone put paper money on the plate as they went. And, I almost forgot, the wearing of black shades was the order of the day!

I am known for not hanging around once I get started, but up in Newton Aycliffe, it was even quicker as they all wanted to get into the pub which was opposite, yet for the same reasons, there were times when not everyone turned up. I had been tipped off that I would receive a public objection to a wedding at the beginning of the service! The problem was that the objector would be the father of the bride who reckoned that the groom was not, "worthy of our lass!" That is not in itself a valid objection and I determined that I would overrule it. I rang up my ever supportive Archdeacon. "What are you going to do?" he chuckled. I told him that I had fixed it with the organist and choir that music would be both played and sung and that I would invite both families to retire to the vestry where I would hear out the objection and then overrule them, come what may. The archdeacon was more than happy, but I didn't have to worry as the father of the bride got himself absolutely drunk as a lord the night before and did not get to the wedding. On another occasion we had the problem that one of the consenting parties might not turn up. It is reasonable to expect that the wedding registers will be made up ready, so that couples do not have to hang around unnecessarily after the tying of the knot. On this day there was another wedding afterwards which I was taking whereas Father Frank was taking the first one. I determined that the copy of the first wedding should be entered into the certificate book and that if there was no wedding, then it could be torn out and destroyed. I was also able to head up the actual weddings, again, because if there was no ceremony, then they could be used for the second wedding. I agreed to hide in the Lady Chapel and wait for the actual declaration that the couple were man and wife, before starting to write up the registers. The couple turned up, the ceremony was legally performed, Father Frank looked nervously in my direction and I started to write, having suggested that he might spin out the prayers a bit. I just about finished as he pronounced the final blessing and as he guided the couple to the writing desk which had been conveniently placed at the end of the choir stalls and adjacent to the Lady Chapel, I held the registers out for him and the couple did not notice!

I have told the stories of two weddings in Newton Aycliffe and I could regale you with lots more, but suffice it to say that in the end I think I have managed to instil into the hearts and minds of couples that what they are about to undertake is not to be done lightly. I know that there have been some who have fallen by the wayside, but there are many that are still together and happy, and with a family. For that I gave hearty thanks to Almighty God. Couples take away with them a candle. They each light a candle during the first hymn which symbolises their separateness, they then light a third candle once they have exchanged their vows. That candle represents their own very unique relationship and I suggest that they bring it out and light it again at the baptism of their first child. A good organist, a faithful choir and verger and the delight of bells, contribute to a memorable occasion for any couple who come to be married.

I have always enjoyed the presence of funeral directors. They have a wonderful sense of humour and if you ever get an invitation to an Undertakers Hop, then make sure that you accept. It can be riotous! In fairness to them, they need to have a good sense of humour or they could not do the job. In Newton Aycliffe, I learned that funerals were taken extremely seriously and you could soon lose friends if things went wrong. I also learned that a type of theatrical drama is played out and you need to be ready for it. Now there was a certain undertaker who was somewhat

Dickensian in all that he did. Others would have said that he was downright unctuous. There was a wringing of hands and a 'yours eventually' attitude! Would Father mind awfully? I got a bit fed up with it, but on one occasion there was no room in the limousine and so I was obsequiously asked if I would mind going in the hearse. One might say that the client was not going to mind. Once inside the hearse, the mask came off and this undertaker turned out to be a real comic and first rate mimic. We roared with laughter as we proceeded down the A1 (M), but as soon as we swept into the crematorium grounds at Darlington, the mask went back on!

The Co-op had the biggest cut of funerals and yet the individual parlours did not always get on with one another. Certainly, Bishop Auckland and Darlington were a case in point, yet on one occasion, Bishop Auckland Co-op had to drop off a family at the Co-operative Tea Rooms in Darlington and I went along as well. It was a step back in time and you might as well have been living in the 20s. Everything was done to a Tee and there was a modest glass of dry sherry served by a waitress in old fashioned uniform. Absolutely classic. I became very friendly with the Co-op at Darlington, but on one occasion, I was sorely tried because as the bearers came out of St. Clare's carrying a coffin, they actually slipped and the coffin dropped. It all happened so quickly that I did not have time to have a heart attack and thank goodness they caught it and order was restored. I muttered to the undertaker that I reckoned they were all, p——— up! He meekly agreed and went bright red. When we got in the car, I asked for a further explanation as clearly they had all been on the booze. Then it came out that local culture demanded it. The undertaker's men were invited in for whisky before the procession to church. Much whisky was poured out and if it was refused, then the Co-op would lose the business!

I also had dealings with a local firm called Meynells. One day I was invited by Alan the boss to go to his house for an evening of snooker. I was talking to one of his men about the invitation and he just said to me rather darkly, "Have a good time, but just make sure he wins." I went along with that! But he proved his worth to me a little later when we had the funeral of a soldier who had been killed by the I.R.A. It was big time and the army turned up in force, but I made sure that they did not take over. My colleague Anne actually took the funeral, and I acted as the go-between and general master of ceremonies. We got to the end of the service so Anne and I went to the back of the church and turned about. It was then that I thought that something horrific would happen as the corporals who were acting as bearers marched in, about turned, and started to pick up the coffin so as to come out head first. Thank goodness that Alan who had been a Staff Sergeant in the Scots Guards was not going to let it go. He just told them to put down the coffin, he then about turned them, got them to lift the coffin and then turned them round so that they came out in the correct manner. I am not really sure if the officers even noticed it!

In Warwickshire, I think that I have dealt mostly with Bennetts of Stratford and Edward Jarvis, known as Ted The Dead and more recently, Hemming and Peace, both of Alcester. I had very happy times with Bennetts, most of the time of which I dealt with Brian who had married Enid Bennett. Brian had served in the Household Cavalry and his back was as straight as a dye. We used to call at the Fox at Loxley on returning from the crematorium near Wellesbourne. On one famous occasion the mourners of the funeral also decided to call and we had a whale of a party. The landlord had served in the S.A.S. and he was a wiry character who had played good rugby in his day. Just after he moved in, the yobs of Stratford decided to pay him a courtesy call. The police heard all about it on the Monday, but they need not have worried, because it had all been sorted out promptly and expeditiously; they never called again. Brian used to use one particular grave digger, but he had a problem in as much that he did not drive, he had to be dropped off at the pub first and then collected from there afterwards. It just so happened that on one particular day, the arrangements went astray and when the funeral party turned up at church, Brian went over to inspect the grave as a normal precaution. He got the shock of his life because all that could be seen was an amount of turf that had been lifted leaving the outline of a coffin lid and nothing else. Clearly our friend had decided to take a break down the pub. Urgent situations require urgent action and so the vicar was taken aside and told that there were to be none of his twenty minutes jobs, but that he had to spin it out for at least 45 minutes. Once the coffin had been carried in, Brian and his men then grabbed some spades, took off their jackets and went to work with a vengeance, only just digging the grave before tidying themselves up and going back into church to bring out the coffin and mourners!

Ted was quite a character and very much into horses, so if we ever had a horse drawn hearse, then he was very much into his element. I remember a big service in church once and Ted had been to the house to collect the family. He came back to warn me that the champagne had been opened and that it was flowing merrily and had been for some time. It certainly helped with the singing. On another occasion we had a funeral followed by interment at the cemetery and once again we had problems with the measurements and I had memories of my first funeral all those years ago. In fairness to Ted, I think that his gravedigger had been a bit tight on the inches. The coffin was placed over the hole and I gave the order to lower it. Then the fun started because basically it only went down a few inches. I looked at Ted and Ted looked at me. What he was trying to say was, Get on with it and do the committal. So I did as I was told and pronounced the prayer. I held my breath. Would the mourners want to come up close to the coffin? Thank God, they didn't and they all walked away, but not before one of them had whispered to Ted, "Well done, I saw that, you handled it well." Some years ago, we both covered a funeral when the coffin was made of cardboard and it began to rain. Horror of horrors and when we arrived at the woodland burial site it was hammering down. Thank goodness the cardboard did not give way! My friends at H & P have only been in business a few years and bring both youth and a few new ideas into the business. No horror stories that directly concern them, but it appears that a few months ago there was a funeral when the screws in the coffin had not made adequate contact and as the coffin lowered into the grave the lid remained at surface level. I hasten to add that it was not their funeral! I also have good memories of Dyers, Thomas Bros, and Bakers and last but not least Jack Clifford the monumental mason from Stratford.

So, I am almost at the end. A priest's ministry is really involved with reconciliation and when serving as a Union Rep I did on one occasion manage to bring the two sides together in a dispute. A full time official came up from London to meet with me and the entire diocesan hierarchy. He was courteous, charming and academically gifted and some of those present were clearly very impressed with his abilities. The problem was solved to much mutual satisfaction and I was congratulated on my diplomacy and negotiating skills. As the union has always said, if there is a strike, then the union has failed.

I would not have wanted to be anything other than a priest. If you push me to an alternative, then I would list four possibilities: undertaker, trade union official, publican and income tax official! The biblically astute amongst you will comment that two of those positions were considered to be sinful. But I must finish, just as I must go at the end of 2012. It is time to go, but it is not time to finish being a priest. I shall remain a priest, (God willing) to my dying day. It has been an unspeakable privilege. I want to thank Hilary above all others for joining me on my pilgrimage which has taken us to all sorts of places. I want to thank so many parishioners who have been both a support and in many cases an inspiration. I have tried to play my best shot, occasionally it has been a very bad shot and I knew it as I played it, but also it has sometimes winged its way to the boundary and the cover drive has been something of beauty, delicacy, power and strength. That was the definition of grace given all those years ago by Bishop John McKie. It is good and like everything that is good, it all comes by and through the Cross of Jesus.

Per Crucem!